SAS INSIDER

HACHETTE MILITARY COLLECTION

Clint Palmer
SAS INSIDER

BY
ROBERT MACKLIN

hachette
AUSTRALIA

All internal photographs are from Clint Palmer's personal collection

hachette
AUSTRALIA

First published in Australia and New Zealand in 2014
by Hachette Australia
(an imprint of Hachette Australia Pty Limited)
Level 17, 207 Kent Street, Sydney NSW 2000
www.hachette.com.au

This edition published in 2015

10 9 8 7 6 5 4 3 2 1

National Library of Australia
Cataloguing-in-Publication data:

Macklin, Robert, author.

SAS insider/Clint Palmer with Robert Macklin.

978 0 7336 3459 8 (paperback)

Palmer, Clint.
Australia. Army. Special Air Service Regiment – Biography.
Soldiers – Australia – Biography.
Soldiers – Training of – Australia.
Parachuting.
War on Terrorism, 2001 – 2009.
Military assistance, Australian – Afghanistan.
Military assistance, Australian – Iraq.

Palmer, Clint.

355.0092

Cover design and illustrations by Luke Causby
Text design by Bookhouse, Sydney
Typeset in Garamond Premier Pro
Printed and bound in Australia by McPherson's Printing Group

MIX
Paper from
responsible sources
FSC® C001695
www.fsc.org

The paper this book is printed on is certified against the Forest Stewardship Council® Standards. McPherson's Printing Group holds FSC® chain of custody certification SA-COC-005379. FSC® promotes environmentally responsible, socially beneficial and economically viable management of the world's forests.

This is for Isabel, Callan and Kelsee
from Clint Palmer

This is for Sami, the wonder girl
from Robert Macklin

CONTENTS

AUTHOR'S NOTE

The SAS operates largely in secrecy. Its official history, *SAS: Phantoms of War*, penned by Professor David Horner, a Duntroon graduate and Colonel in the Army Reserve, presents only those aspects of its activities that the Regiment and the Army's high command have cleared for public consumption. This is easily justifiable on the grounds that the SAS is at the cutting edge of our military capability and to reveal too much of its methods and tactics would not be just counterproductive, it would add immeasurably to the dangers faced by the SAS soldiers in the field.

But it does mean that the human face of the SASR is almost as invisible to the public as those of its current operatives, whose identities are closely guarded. So when the opportunity arose to tell the story of Clint Palmer, who had spent 28 years – literally half his lifetime – as a key member of the Regiment, rising to the rank of Warrant Officer Class One and with experience in most aspects of its operations, I was more than happy to accept the challenge.

It was not my first close encounter with the SAS. In 2010 I had worked closely and harmoniously with one of the Regiment's top marksmen, the recently retired Rob Maylor, to produce the bestselling book *SAS Sniper*, later published in America as *Sniper Elite*. In the process I had developed a firm friendship with Rob and his family which endures to this day and had met other serving members of the regiment in a social setting.

However, it was publication of that book which triggered an email from a third party suggesting that Clint, who had recently retired, had led such a remarkable life within the SAS that his story demanded to be told. And while I had no doubt that his personal journey would be thoroughly absorbing (as indeed it turned out to be), I was just as interested in taking the opportunity it afforded to reflect upon the development of the SAS itself. So I contacted Clint, flew to Perth a couple of times and developed a *modus operandi* that would permit him to tell the personal story in his own words but would allow me to place it in the larger context of the Regiment's own biography.

This entailed a return to the very foundations of Special Forces operations and the creation of the British SAS in

World War II. I then uncovered through various sources the remarkably informal and behind-the-scenes birth of the Australian equivalent in 1957, coincidentally the same year that Clint himself first drew breath. This led to a fascinating path of growth and continual reformation as the Regiment responded to the changing circumstances of Australia's defence posture.

Its early experience in Malaya and Borneo – in league with the British SAS – followed by the Vietnam War as part of an American-led mission, lay the foundations of the Regiment's 'green' capabilities: jungle warfare combining reconnaissance and surveillance missions with ambush and firefight contacts with the enemy. Then came the rise of guerrilla warfare and terrorism and the SASR responded with a 'black' counter-terrorism (CT) capability that drew it into that shadowy world where military and espionage circles intersect.

The conflicts in the Middle East where the set battles of the 20th century were replaced by insurgent outbreaks fuelled by religious extremism meant that the West's Special Forces would inevitably take a lead role with the Australian SAS more than willing to play its part in that coalition. And on the new battlefield it proved its worth time and time again. However, while this brought a growing prestige within the ADF and raised morale inside the Regiment, it also attracted the attention and admiration of politicians, notably

Prime Minister John Howard. This led to the unfortunate involvement of the SAS in the so-called Tampa Affair, which brought in its train a public perception of refugees as an enemy force to be resisted by the elite of our armed forces. There is some evidence that it also alerted the regimental leadership to the need to temper it's 'can do' attitude at the fringe of the political arena. If so, it was a lesson well learned.

More recently there have been revelations that the Regiment's activities have extended to Africa and that an element of its operational forces has established a working relationship with the Australian Security Intelligence Service. Neither development should come as a surprise. The terrorist threats to Australia's security know no continental bounds and any prudent defence planner would include the politically turbulent African experience within the area of long-range reconnaissance and surveillance.

However, in my exploration of the regiment's development it has never been my intention to seek out or to reveal operational secrets that would endanger our soldiers in the field or to hinder their anonymity at home or aboard. Instead I hope that I have used this element as intended – to provide a context for the journey of one man through the ups and downs of a career in the most demanding environment available to an Australian soldier.

In doing so I have been greatly assisted by Professor Horner's excellent book, which provided the bedrock for my research; to many other researchers in the field in the United States, the UK and not least among the Australians, Ian McPhedran's *The Magnificent SAS* and Sandra Lee's *18 Hours*.

Throughout I was greatly encouraged and supported by my publisher Matthew Kelly at Hachette Australia and my gratitude is unbounded. My thanks are also due to my friend and colleague Peter Thompson, and especially to my wife, Wendy, who had to endure the emotional travails that accompany the research and writing of this and all my books.

Robert Macklin
Canberra
www.robertmacklin.com

NOTE TO THE READER FROM CLINT PALMER

This book is a story about me – but obviously I cannot tell all there is to know about me and my life. For those who know me well – the people in my life, and those whose lives I have been a part of – you will know that despite the complex nature of my life, I am a simple man who prefers to live simply. As a child growing up in a large family and in the relative isolation of the tropical north, I learned quickly how to amuse myself and take care of myself. The open spaces and freedom of movement afforded me many great opportunities which taught me to be resilient and tougher than the average Australian. As time passed, the basic survival skills I learned as a kid provided a firm foundation for what was to become an unusual career. My parents were both products of the working class, so there wasn't much room for negotiation when it came to pulling your weight around the house. Everyone had their assigned chores and getting them done was the priority before you took off for the day.

Structure and a sense of order were the order of the day in the Palmer household. My father insisted that there were rules for everything; and after the family's needs were met my mother had little time for anything else. Despite the lean circumstances in which we were brought up, we had many opportunities that money simply could not buy. Life in the Northern Territory was interrupted by a brief stint in Brisbane, which may have been an attempt to reunite us with the greater family group, but due to lack of opportunity, my father hauled the family back to the Territory where work paid well and we all were more comfortable.

But all good things come to an end, and that meant a new start in Kalgoorlie. It was a tough and competitive environment for a bunch of kids who were used to dominating a small town. Again, the learning curve was steep but we survived. The only casualty was poor old Dad, moving from job to job. In the end it was to the Pilbara region and a fly-in fly-out job while Mum set up house in Perth. By then I was long gone, and forging my own way in the Australian Army.

My early days as a soldier were difficult. I was young and inexperienced, and so I struggled to maintain a spot in the fast moving game of adulthood. There were many clashes, hard knocks and all-out brawls, which were to test me time and time again. I held my own, lost a couple and then started winning. I knew then that I was well settled in a testosterone-saturated workplace, where you are only as good as your last mistake.

In 1984 my career in the Army took a deviation that was far more challenging, more competitive and more complex than anything I had encountered previously. What turned out to be a 30-year relationship with the Special Air Service was, quite frankly, more than I ever imagined was possible for me. The stakes were suddenly much, much higher.

There were many changes as the family grew up. The one thing that did not change was the unwavering love that my mother had for us all, despite the different directions we all took. That was a constant. Sadly, Mum left us far too prematurely. In 1987, at just 54 years old she succumbed to that ruthless and indiscriminate killer – cancer. For the first time in his life, I think my father was left feeling vulnerable and inadequate. Isabel was the engine room of the family, and suddenly she was gone, Terry never really recovered from that. Yes, he tried to press on, but now he was dealing with all the issues of running a household and maintaining a job, and there was a big gap; a gap which remained with him until his passing in 2013.

The Special Air Service Regiment was now the dominant partner in my life. I had committed to it, and was determined to serve in its embrace for as long as it allowed me. I was now in a different place, amongst the few who had earned the rite of passage, sinking my teeth into all that came before me and relishing every moment. As time passed, I fell in love and married. My treasured children came along and there was now my own family to consider.

The SAS part of my journey has ended, as all journeys do. I have learned so much about myself and my capacity to function in so many ways. I have learned about people and how they are able to bring out the best in you or nearly destroy you. I have learned about love and sadness, about aggression, humility, compassion, loyalty and integrity. There are many emotions that collectively shape our personalities, and over time, as we mature, we understand the gravity of all we have said and done.

I take great pride in reflecting on my time in the SAS. After all these years, I am yet to meet a more dedicated, professional, innovative and loyal group of people than those whom I had the pleasure to serve with – the men of the Special Air Service Regiment.

Clint Palmer

1

OPERATION ANACONDA

SAS Warrant Officer Clint Palmer knew he was about to die.

The rocket-propelled grenade came screaming out of the mountain directly at him . . . death on wings. Half a second seemed like an age. Then it dipped and smashed into the soft earth just ahead of him. There was a big thud and a splash of muddy ground and snow, then a hissing of the propellant, which was still burning. Against all odds, it failed to explode. There was a nanosecond of blessed relief before the al-Qaeda and Taliban fighters opened up with blistering machine-gun and rifle fire from the high ground.

'Bullets started whizzing past my body,' he says. 'I could feel the wind of them. I was just waiting for one of them to hit. I thought I was going to die, out there in the middle of nowhere.'

He started to run. He and his radio operator Jock Wallace, together with the Americans who had exited the Chinook helicopter with him, made a dash for the nearest available cover, a little rocky ledge about 50 metres away. Rifle in one hand, a 15-kilogram pack on his back, helmet, body armour, ammunition, personal radio, heavy boots, assorted gear and weaponry all fought against his desperate need to reach the ledge. 'There was only one way we could go so we just ran for it, ran, scrambling over these rocks and shit going everywhere.

'The clarity of the realisation that this is fair dinkum kicked in. And when you actually smell the rounds and you feel them going past you that's when you hope like hell it doesn't get worse. I'm not a religious man but I had faith in somebody to look after me at that point in time, I tell you.

'After some time of running and nothing had hit and I was feeling all this movement in the air around me I told myself, "No way, I am not going to die." But the initial sensation was, "I'm fucked."'

At last, he reached the ledge and threw himself over it. Bullets and RPGs continued to rain down. 'We started yelling at everyone else to take cover,' he says. Some of the American troops who'd been in the Chinooks with them had dropped their packs in a mad dash for cover. Some had been hit. There were screams and curses punctuating the clatter of fire from above and ricochets from the rocks. But as he searched the surrounding heights for targets through the reflex sight on his M4 there was a moment to take stock.

It was all bad.

When the RPG hit, he'd been in a group of Americans that included Lieutenant Colonel Paul LaCamera, the commanding officer of the 1-87th Infantry Regiment, and his Command Sergeant Major, Frank Grippe. Clint had come up against both of them in the days leading up to the battle. He'd immediately hit it off with his fellow senior NCO Grippe (pronounced Grippy). 'Good man, Frank,' he says. They would become mates, their friendship tempered in the hell of being isolated, surrounded by a fierce enemy and under fire for 14 hours straight. That either welds men together or sparks a simmering hatred that never dies. Palmer and Grippe certainly welded.

There was already tension between Palmer and LaCamera when the Chinooks that would take them into the biggest battle of the Afghan War – Operation Anaconda – took off from Bagram airbase three hours before. And at first glance it seems incongruous. In the military scheme of things, lieutenant colonels so outrank sergeant majors that conflict is preposterous. Not so in this instance. The two men came from different worlds.

LaCamera was the ambitious battalion commander in the big army out to make a name for himself. And unlike so many of his compatriots, the West Pointer had no love for Australians, especially of the non-commissioned class. Clint Palmer, a stocky 45, came from an elite Australian unit where officers passed through on their journey up the ladder, but where the NCOs stayed in place.

'LaCamera would preside over a battalion headquarters brief and he'd dominate,' Palmer says. 'He'd sit on a chair in the middle of the room while his boys went sir this, sir that. I'm standing at the back thinking, "Is there any wonder there's tension here, or flaws in the plan – inefficient passage of information; inefficient briefing procedures?" The soldiers were no wiser as to what was going on five days out as they were when they were on the ground. In my world we don't do it that way.'

Then came a series of events that added a whole new dimension to the mix. And to understand them we must take a couple of steps back in time.

Anaconda was launched on 2 March 2002. It came in the wake of the Tora Bora disaster in early December 2001, when the Americans and their Afghan allies allowed the al-Qaeda leadership to slip through their net. On 22 December the Taliban government fell to the Northern Alliance and Hamid

Karzai was installed as acting president in Kabul, only three months after the tragedy of 9/11.

In January 2002, US Special Forces had discovered an al-Qaeda training area in the Shahi-Kot Valley, high in the mountainous Hindu Kush bordering Pakistan and south of Tora Bora. They suspected the leadership might be there, maybe even Osama bin Laden himself. If they could take it out they would regain the face they had lost at Tora Bora, and with a bit of luck they'd wrap the whole Afghan venture up and return to a ticker-tape parade down Broadway.

They devised a battle plan. Anaconda would be the biggest combat operation since Vietnam and it would be conducted at an unprecedented altitude of 8,000 feet, right at the edge of a soldier's fighting capability. It would be a classic 'hammer and anvil' strategy. For geopolitical reasons they would use a force element of Afghans under the charge of American Special Forces as the hammer. They would drive in and smash the enemy from the north-west while LaCamera's troops, the anvil, took up a blocking position in the south-east to round up or take out the survivors as they fled.

By now Prime Minister John Howard – who had been in Washington on 9/11 – had committed Australia to the conflict and Australia's SAS Commanding Officer Lieutenant Colonel 'Gus' Gilmore and his operations officer, Major Pete Tinley, had travelled to the American Middle East theatre command to 'sell' the SAS. As Gilmore told News Limited's defence writer Ian McPhedran, he and Tinley would spend weeks lobbying the Americans for a central role in the Afghan operation.[1]

They made the sale. In Anaconda the hammer was seeded with an Australian SAS unit (1 Squadron) while another SAS patrol had an overwatch position high up in the south-west. Palmer and his radio operator were embedded with LaCamera's battalion. It was a job he relished. Despite his 19 years' service in the SASR confronting a range of life-threatening hazards, this was his first opportunity to engage an enemy in combat. But while he welcomed the soldier's ultimate proving ground, he was trained to minimise risks to himself and his compatriots. And by the time that RPG headed his way he'd already been engaged in a series of tactical disputes.

Until the eve of battle, all the intelligence briefings had put the enemy force at Shahi-Kot at between 150 and 250 fighters. But suddenly new information arrived (in part from the SAS) that raised the figure exponentially. Palmer was among only seven soldiers at the briefing given by the top American commander of the operation, General Frank 'Buster' Hagenback. He says, 'Hagenback said, "Look, sit down guys. This is bigger than we thought. There's going to be up to 1,500 bad guys out there . . ."'

This put an entirely new focus on the risks to the southern insertion force. The planners had designated landing zones (LZs) on the valley floor where, in the absence of any real resistance, there was plenty of room for the choppers to manoeuvre. 'I'm going, "holy shit," he says. 'I went straight down to my commander and I told him.

"I said there's still time to change the plan".' All it required, Palmer says, 'was to come in on the ridgeline, take them by surprise and if there's resistance we hit 'em with everything, knock 'em out and we've got the high ground.'

'I think I even said, "Have you ever heard of the book *Bear Trap*? This is exactly what the Russians did and they got a battalion of helicopter-borne troops wiped out doing the same things".'

When they did land the enemy was indeed taken by surprise. Two Chinooks, each carrying about 40 American soldiers and the two Australians, arrived at their LZs on schedule at 6.04 a.m. Initial resistance was nil. They spread out and began moving up the valley. All was quiet in the cold, clear morning air. No wind and an eerie silence as they walked from the choppers, the silence of anticipation, the absolute certainty that something was about to occur. Clint looked up. The sky was blue and cool, some whiskers of cloud high up, but otherwise clear. The sun was bright but not hot, the snow scattered across the ground ahead.

However, the Americans walking ahead of them soon spotted figures on a ridgeline to the west and instantly opened fire. The Australian ran forward. In the briefing he'd been told that a unit of six American SEALs designated Mako 31 was in that position and would be displaying a VS-17 marker. And sure enough, there it was. The Americans were firing on their compatriots. 'When our helicopter came in I saw them, three of them standing there,' he says. 'We flew right past them. I knew what was going on. The headquarters knew they were there – "If you see guys up to the left, they're ours. They're friendly, don't open up on them." But the information hadn't trickled down.' Everything Palmer had feared was happening. He shouted, 'Stop, stop, stop! They're friendly; stop shooting; hold your fire!'

The Americans looked around. The Australian Warrant Officer's voice had the authority of command. They put down their weapons. The SEALs slipped away unharmed. Ten minutes into the operation and already there'd been a blue-on-blue.

Before they'd landed in the Chinooks, the American Air Force was supposed to have unleashed a carpet bombing of the entire perimeter of Shahi-Kot's defensive positions – the caves, the mountain redoubts, the training facilities – for a full 55 minutes. This would have devastated the fighting force of Chechens, Mongols, Arabs, Pakistanis and Afghans identified by the Special Forces operators in the days leading up to the battle.

But by this time there were so many operational commands (from Florida to Qatar to Kuwait to Bagram Airbase) and so many different – and jealously non-communicative – SF units (from the CIA to Delta Force, SEALs, British SAS and the Australians), to say nothing of the competing American mainstream forces wanting a piece of the action, that somehow the Air Force operation got lost in translation. In the event, only one B-1 bomber arrived and dropped a total of six bombs along a humpback ridgeline known as the Whale. The raid lasted a mere five minutes. It did little more than rouse the defenders from their beds deep within the mountain caves.

The Americans did, however, score a couple of knockout punches from the air a little further afield. The 'hammer' force – including a small SAS detachmen – went to war in Afghan trucks salvaged by the Delta teams when their own vehicles proved unsuitable. The Afghan commander, Zia Lodin, had begun the combat operation – his first – with great enthusiasm. He and his ragtag group of about 80 men had been trained for the previous few weeks by their US Special Forces handlers at a compound near the sizeable town of Gardez. Their journey to the battle space so far had been an ordeal. The roads were almost impassable, the trucks barely sprung, but they had endured. Zia had been dismayed by the pipsqueak pre-dawn sortie of the single bomber. But his Special Forces allies reassured him that all would be well when they reached the battleground.

Suddenly mortar rounds began to explode among the convoy. Not only had they been spotted by the al-Qaeda forces in Shahi-Kot, but they had waited until the Afghans had reached a tight, vulnerable position before launching their attack. Zia and his men tried to fight back but the enemy was well concealed. Then, without warning, an American AC-130 gunship, 'Grim 3–1', wildly off course and 10,000 feet above the convoy, attacked his force with its 105 mm Howitzer. Firing eight to 10 massive rounds with pinpoint accuracy, the attack threw Zia's unit into total chaos, smashing trucks, killing several of his men and mortally wounding one American, Chief Warrant Officer Stanley L. Harriman. (The SAS men escaped unscathed.)

The American military PR machine has claimed that Harriman was killed by enemy mortar fire. However, independent sources including the account by author Sean Naylor, who was embedded with Hagenback's force, are in no doubt he was a blue-on-blue casualty.

Palmer agrees. 'There's always an "official" record which is designed to maintain the integrity and professional reputation of a unit in times of war,' he says. 'Unless the mistakes are such that the effects are unquestionably the result of poor tactical decisions or planning and bad leadership, then the public are only told of the generic outcomes which suit the current political environment.

'It is my belief that Stan Harriman died of wounds as the result of fratricide. I spoke to a number of the operators involved in the action, and I also saw the vehicle in which he was travelling after it was recovered and the damage was significant; in my view more than an enemy mortar would inflict.'

The surviving Delta operators tried to rally the Afghans but Zia had had quite enough. He and his men went home.

The hammer was no more.

In the south-east, LaCamera's anvil was now stuck in an indefensible valley.

SAS Warrant Officer Clint Palmer was in more trouble than he knew.

2

HELL'S HALFPIPE

The Americans called it Hell's Halfpipe. It was about 15 metres across and 60 metres long, a bowl in the valley floor. Looking ahead, Clint Palmer could see the bold eminence of the Whale where the al-Qaeda and Taliban forces were well dug in. Beside and beyond that were a series of abandoned compounds and the village of Marzak. On both sides, the mountains reared up in a series of ridgelines and caves perfectly positioned to rain down small arms fire on the 82 men of LaCamera's anvil, including Palmer and his 'chook' (SAS slang for radio operator) Jock Wallace.

Their only cover were the ledges on both sides of the bowl and the rocks that protruded from the soft, moist earth of the waterless creek line carved by centuries of rain and snow rushing down from the peaks.

'We were the target,' Palmer says. 'We were the shooting gallery.'

Then came the mortars. The first round landed 400 metres away, directly south in the valley floor. 'Everyone stopped and looked at each other in horror,' he says. 'They knew exactly what it was. The dynamics of the battle had just changed for the worse.'

Twenty-five seconds later the shout came from half a dozen throats: 'Mortars incoming . . . mortars!' The second round landed 200 metres along the same line, heading straight for them. They mentally counted down the same time lapse for the third round, which landed about 25 metres to the south and just outside the Halfpipe.

'The fourth round impacted right in the middle of the position and between Jock and me,' he says. They were about 15 metres apart. Luckily they were unharmed. The soft wet ground allowed the missiles to bury themselves before they exploded, thereby muffling the impact. 'From then on, every 15 to 20 minutes we would receive a barrage of up to 20 rounds,' he says. 'You could hear the base plate position firing the rounds in the distance, and we knew that 23 seconds later, rounds would be landing. Guys were scurrying from one place to another to dodge incoming rounds. Knowing that one of these things might land on top of you was the most vulnerable I have ever felt.'

As bullets whined overhead, Palmer dug like hell, first with his hands, then with an entrenching tool – a small fold-up shovel – from the abandoned pack of a wounded American. The Americans too were hurriedly digging in to lower their exposure to the explosions. 'It was a frantic time,' he says.

While he dug he realised that the mortars must have been 'walked in' by an al-Qaeda observer hiding in the rocks with a radio. He searched the area. 'There was a cave dug into the side of this hill and the mortar base plate was up in the cave mouth,' he says.

'I crawled forward. I saw the bad guy stuck out there beside a little mud hut structure. I was about 80 metres from him and he saw me and ducked back around the corner. I waited for him to reappear, five minutes, ten, but nothing. So I went back, told LaCamera and they took an AT4 rocket forward to knock him out. When I briefed him to use the AT4 to neutralize the spotter position, others wanted to use it to take out what they thought was a sniper position a greater distance away. They ignored the fact that its range would not be sufficient. It was the only AT4 we had and that young fellow handling it shot the thing about 20 metres above his head ... wasted ... !'

The cave itself was behind significant rock cover. 'You couldn't actually shoot straight into it,' he says, 'and even the jets that came later couldn't drop bombs into the mouth of the cave because of the angle of the location. So for the rest of the day, they were just pounding us from the top.'

With the mortars came the screams of men hit by deadly shrapnel.

'We were pulling them into cover – the holes we had dug – and doing what we could for them,' he says. 'There was a little knoll where the American 120 mortar crew had set up and one landed among these blokes. There were 10 of them, and it was just like the movies when they were thrown through the air. One round landed right between the legs of the boss of the mortars and stripped all the meat off both his legs. He was in the hurt locker. They grabbed him and ran him towards us. We were giving him covering fire as they brought him in. The doc strapped him up, and we tried to stop the bleeding as best we could. Later that day when I had my hole deep enough, he went in the hole.'

One of the Americans giving covering fire was shot in the foot. 'He rolled down the hill to me, screaming,' Palmer says. 'It was now very clear that we were in deep shit – dominated by high ground on either flank and a village [Marzak] 700 metres to the north with a couple of hundred bad guys in it.'

The eight wounded were laid out in the centre and to the south of the inner part of the Halfpipe. 'They were very vulnerable to further attack,' Palmer says. 'As the mortars continued during the day many of the wounded came very close to being injured a second time . . . and some were.'

The American radio operators were further up the Halfpipe near LaCamera. But they had a problem. 'When the mortar fire started, one of those radios – they had two – was damaged,' he says. 'The antenna system was blown up so it wouldn't transmit or receive properly. And the other radio may not have been able to reach base because one was VHF and the other was HF – the HF got whacked. So they had no comms back to the battalion for hours in the morning. Amidst the confusion and intermittent messages it was nearly two hours into the battle before we knew the real and more complete picture.'

That was when he discovered that the 'hammer' was no longer a factor in the battlespace. It meant not only that Anaconda had ceased to be a viable operation but that the enemy was released from the defence of its northern flank and could concentrate its fire on the 'anvil'. From that point the Allies were on a hiding to nothing.

The casualties were mounting quickly. It was vital to get word out. He looked around for Wallace. 'He was located probably 10 to 15 metres from me,' Palmer says. 'You spread out, otherwise one hit from a mortar kills both of us. But every now and then when it was appropriate, I'd get up and move real quick to where he was with the radio.' At about 7.45 he made a situation report (sitrep) back to base.

This was the one bright spot in the desperate confusion – the Australians had a good clear signal from their radio back to Bagram. 'We had TACSAT (tactical satellite communications), so we were talking straight back to Tink, who was relaying the messages to Hagenbeck,' he says. 'That was keeping Hagenbeck up to date because he was getting nothing out of the Brigade command net.

'So Hagenbeck, left the [American] TOC (tactical operation) and came into our TOC and was sitting there listening to me talking on the radio giving live updates.' However, it was just this apparent asset that would cause some of the most bitter contention in a day of raw nerves and violent conflict, not least between the Australian warrant officer and the American commander.

There was an urgent need to evacuate the seriously wounded. 'The mortar boss got hit 7 to 7.30 in the morning,' Palmer says. 'He and another guy who was hit quite badly were just bleeding away.' So for the first of several times that day he went forward to LaCamera. 'One: what's going on?' he said, 'Two, how can I help? Three, I can help because I've got TACSAT – good clear comms.'

LaCamera was not receptive.

In fact LaCamera desperately wanted air cover. They had started the operation with helicopter gunships in support but they soon departed to refuel. Finally two returned just before 8 a.m. and opened fire on enemy positions called in by Frank Grippe's battalion air support officer. But now they attracted intense fire from the al-Qaeda and Taliban fighters hidden in the caves and level with them. 'One of them was right above us when it got hit on the nose with an RPG,' Palmer says. 'I thought, "Hell, this thing is going to fall on top of us." That was pretty amazing, but it took off and next time we saw one was 3.30 to 4 o'clock in the afternoon.'

The Americans kept trying for air cover, and finally one of their radio operators was able to call in a B-52 bomber. However, no sooner had he made contact than his radio went down and he turned to the Australians for help. Jock handed over their radio and the American called in the coordinates. When Clint heard them, he says he immediately felt 'something didn't compute.'

'I don't know what it was,' he says, 'I just knew the information they sent the aircraft was wrong. He was just about to give the execution signal and I yelled out, "Stop, stop, stop! Correction, correction. Wait out."

As it happened, one of his SAS colleagues back at Bagram had offered him his small GPS unit to take into the field. 'I got the GPS out and checked it. "Bugger me," I said, "you've just given the aircraft [an order] to drop the bombs on us!"

'I did a quick calculation. The enemy were 300 metres to the east, so I gave the new grid numbers and he called through the correction to the aircraft.' The pilot responded,

"New grid confirmed . . . okay, inbound . . . bomb doors opened . . . bombs gone".'

Palmer says, 'Twenty-four seconds later all hell broke loose – 50 250-pound dumb bombs hit. It was deafening. They hit the target spot on. They landed right on the ridge line . . . awesome. The fighters had whipped back into their holes but they would have been shell shocked. However, it wasn't long before they got into us again . . .'

Of the 82 soldiers in the defending force, 15 were dropped 2 kilometres ahead of the main body. 'They were headed by a Special Forces captain,' he says, 'and they were contacting and engaging bad guys all day long. They were running up and down creek lines, ambushing and engaging them as they were coming down to get us. So they were a help to us, disorganising them.'

Occasionally the US radio operators were able to call in air support. Soon after 11 a.m. an F-15 screamed into the valley on a bombing raid. However, the enemy was prepared. 'It dropped a couple of bombs,' Palmer says, 'and a SAM missile went up its arse; the aircraft fired its chaff, rolled and turned away and the missile blew up in the chaff. The Yanks got up shouting, "Yeah . . . kick arse!" but when the shots came in they hit the ground. It was quite spectacular. That was about the only incident of a SAM missile being fired in the Afghan conflict.'

Most of the enemy fire was coming from a ridgeline about 300 metres away. 'Every weapon system we had was able to engage quite effectively out that far,' he says, 'but there was a heavier machine-gun in another ridgeline above that and we didn't have anything that could reach it.' LaCamera sent a small team – four to six American troops – up the slope to check out its location. 'They were ordered to get up on the high ground and see what they could see,' Clint says. But they were spotted and the result was a squad of fighters stuck up there most of the day.

This added to the frustration that was simmering just beneath the surface in the Australian's dealings with the American commander.

There were occasions when the shooting died and nothing was happening, but never for very long. 'The engagement was sustained over a long period of time and that's what makes the day so significant,' Palmer says. 'The amount of fire was uncanny. It tended to reinforce the belief that there were a lot of people out there. These guys do not carry a lot on them, so there was either not so many people with a lot of ammunition or there were a lot of people with other people bringing ammunition forward to sustain fire. I think the latter is how it went because we saw a lot of movement periodically. And during the day as things escalated it appeared, simply by the volume of fire we were receiving, that the pace was growing, and the attacks becoming more frequent and heavier.'

Lunchtime came and went. The two Australians had brought American MREs (meals ready to eat), but neither gave them a second thought. 'I didn't eat or drink the whole day,' Palmer says. 'Too much going on. I didn't think about it.'

Occasionally the battle would be punctuated by the arrival of a US B-1 bomber delivering JDAMs (joint direct action munition bombs) at the ridgelines. And in the silence that followed the percussion came the groans and whimpers from the wounded in the Halfpipe. By now Palmer had three in his hole and there was no room for him to take cover. He returned time and again to his radioman, who got Colonel Tink on the line.

Back at the Bagram base, General Hagenbeck decided the engagement had reached a stalemate of two equal and opposing forces. That was not Clint's perception at all. And throughout the afternoon the al-Qaeda and Taliban were raising the tempo of the battle. 'We were taking a huge amount of fire,' he says. 'It built up gradually through the day and it was like a crescendo.'

During a lull, Frank Grippe stood up and came back through the Halfpipe. 'He was trying to rally the troops,' Clint says. 'He went around saying, "How are you going, man? Hang in there. How are you doin' dude?" Frank was good like that.' But then a mortar went off behind him. 'It dug a hole in his arse cheek,' Palmer says. 'I was quite close to him. A couple of rounds came in and he and LaCamera got up and ran slightly up the bowl; and when they moved the next round came in right behind them. If they hadn't moved they'd have been all right. He moved straight into it.'

The sense of isolation was adding to Palmer's frustration. He was getting little feedback from his commander at Bagram. The one shaft of sunlight came from his SAS colleague Grant Mason, who was observing the action with his 1 Squadron troop on a mountain further to the west.

'In mid-afternoon, when it was getting really heavy, he rang me direct from there. He said, "Hey, hang in there, mate," all that and, "Stick with it and we'll see you when you get back." That was a big morale booster. You've got no idea how much, because at the end of the day, we felt totally isolated and because we were not getting any positive support back from headquarters there was a feeling of abandonment. It was terrific to get that little bit of bloody reinforcement . . . positive reinforcement . . . no other prick did.'

By now the incoming crescendo was reaching its peak. 'It was like the last-ditch effort for the day and they were going to dislodge us,' he says. 'It was between 4 and 4.30 in the afternoon.' Then Palmer too was hit by shrapnel – the radio was smashed, though he was unhurt. 'The last mortar round that went off that day landed only about 2 metres away from me,' he says. 'The noise was deafening. My pack, which was on the ground in front of me, went flying behind me. I was flattened. When I got up there was a hole in the ground and I couldn't find my pack. I rolled over and my pack was 5 or 10 metres behind me. Pure luck.'

It took out the personal radio lodged in his body armour. 'The radio was for comms between Jock and I,' he says, 'and also it was on the same frequency as the Australians [from 1 Squadron] if they had come down the valley. I'd have been able to talk to them on that.

'I didn't use it at all. When I tried to do the radio check, it didn't work so I turned it off. I didn't even realise I had been hit. The radio had taken some shrapnel but I didn't realise till afterwards.'

The volume of fire was now greater than it had been throughout the day. 'Tracer flew overhead from the east,' he says. 'Seconds later rounds cracked in from the west. Now soldiers were being engaged from both sides and from high positions. As I lay there, rounds thumped into the rocks and ground around us and then in quick succession one, two, three, four men were shot – in the foot, hand and leg, thigh, another in the leg. They didn't realise they had been shot at from behind until they were hit. Both flanks then collapsed and everyone rolled forward down into the middle of a small gully – 82 men in the shit! Almost on cue, small arms fire opened up from the north. Frank and I lay on our backs, eyes wide open, looking at the wall of tracer slicing a three-way hatch over our heads. Everything seemed louder and closer. One could sense this was potentially, the "last stand". This intense fire lasted 20 to 25 minutes, and stopped as suddenly as it began, almost as though someone was controlling it.'

At 5.30 'It was noisy, then nothing. We wondered what was going on. And it was about that time that some of the bad guys were coming down off the ridge and they were heading back up to Marzak. That was when LaCamera said, "Fuck, I want Marzak to disappear." Those were his exact words: "I want Marzak to disappear". So he called in an attack bomber – a B-1 bomber, 10 JDAMs, boom, boom, boom, flattened the valley. All that was left was matchsticks and dust and bits of meat flying everywhere. Awesome – that's "shock and awe". That was right towards the end of the day.'

But by no means was it the end of the battle.

3

EVERY MAN FOR HIMSELF

The last overwhelming burst of fire took its toll. At least eight Americans had been wounded and put out of action. 'It was almost unbelievable that no one was killed outright,' Palmer says. The final count would be 30 wounded, 16 seriously injured – two critically or gravely ill. 'They'd had to wait all day just bleeding away,' he says. 'They had no blood; they were grey just like death warmed up, barely clinging on.'

Despite the urgent need to get the casualties to hospital the American command had been unwilling to send medivac helicopters to their stricken men. 'They were afraid of losing a helicopter,' Palmer says. 'And now they couldn't decide whether to reinforce us or evacuate.'

As darkness fell, the enemy had consolidated its positions to the east, west and north of the Halfpipe. As the shadows of the huge mountains fell across the valley floor the air quickly turned bitingly cold. No snow fell that day but with every passing hour the cold would deepen and their position would become harder to hold. The only way out was through the south. 'That wasn't an option at that point because we were there to stay,' Palmer says. 'And that's why, later in the evening, the al-Qaeda fighters infiltrated round the back towards the south.' While RPG fire continued from the high ground, about 30 fighters headed around behind them.

'They were swinging around to the south-east and were going to come up and squeeze us,' he says. 'That would have been the first step of the pincer and the demolition of our force because that was the most vulnerable approach to us. From the south you look straight up into the Halfpipe at ground level. It was on the same plane. So if they got down there with their RPGs and opened up on us then we would have been in deep trouble.' Fortunately they were spotted and an AC-130 gunship that had just arrived on station opened up on them. 'No question – that AC-130 saved our lives.'

At least for the moment . . . but prospects were uniformly grim. While the AC-130 had temporarily scattered the 30 fighters, killing many of them, there was still a powerfully active force holding its ground above the Halfpipe. 'We had a lot of RPGs coming in during the evening,' he says. 'We were ambushed. We had gone straight into the jaws of the bad guys.'

He asked Jock Wallace to connect him with Lieutenant Colonel Tink. 'I gave him an update and I said, "It's bad; this is a major assault happening."' If they were not withdrawn by first light in the morning they would probably be coming out in body bags. 'I told Tink that we required medivac straight away for the wounded guys. And if so, I wanted to know what was the aircraft that was coming in. If it was a CH-47, then there would be enough space for us both.' Since his job was finished – as indeed it had been since the hammer and anvil plan fell over 10 hours previously – he asked whether there would be room for Wallace and himself to be withdrawn at the same time. The conversation was punctuated by machine-gun fire from the Americans, the groans of the wounded pleading for morphine and the low thump of RPGs exploding.

Tink replied, 'Are you wounded?'

Palmer: 'No. But it's only a matter of time before we are.'

Tink: 'If you're not a casualty you're to stay in place.'

Palmer: 'Roger. Understood.'

Tink: 'Dig in.'

Jock Wallace says, 'Clint was fully aware that he had my life as well as his own to look after. We had been on the ground all day . . . we'd had casualties for over eight hours when this was occurring and Clint had had enough. He just said this is crap and he told them in no uncertain terms.'[2]

He ended the call and turned to Wallace. If they were going to be overrun, their duty was to activate an E&E (escape and evasion) plan. This was an essential element of their training procedure, one that he had pounded home to young recruits. 'I said to Jock, "Mate, if this all goes to shit and we get overrun and we've got no choice and have to withdraw, we're going to head down south then up west and try to locate 1 Squadron".'

Wallace agreed.

However, Palmer's outburst to his task force commander – which he reinforced in two further sitreps over the next hour – might well have had its effect at the command post. Tink made representations to Hagenbeck, who decided to send in the medivac choppers: two specially modified Black Hawks.

'They were firing at us with RPGs when the medivac helicopters came in,' Palmer says. 'They were trying to shoot the helicopters out of the sky with RPGs. We had to get the wounded out to the helos, and that meant we had to carry them, physically pick them up and carry them, three or four trips there and back under RPG fire from the same guys who were trying to get around behind us.' The two critically injured soldiers were in bad shape. 'They were probably five minutes, 10 minutes from death by the time they got them back to the hospital. They were so lucky. Their pulses were so weak. They got stabilised and sent straight to Germany.' The stretcher cases went aboard; the walking wounded stayed. The issue for the Australians now was whether the Allied force could hold out through a freezing night as a reinforced al-Qaeda and Taliban enemy closed in. But once again, it would seem, Clint's sitreps were bearing fruit. Now Rowan Tink broke with Hagenbeck's fanciful notion that they were dealing with a 'stalemate'.[3]

Tink said later, 'They did not have that sort of information [as received from Palmer]; they were surprised when I went over and gave it to them.'

It may well be that without Palmer's forceful intervention, the 'stalemate' doctrine would have prevailed. In the light of subsequent events, this is highly significant. However, it would not be until midnight – 18 hours after they had landed on the valley floor that morning – that the two Chinooks arrived to extract them and the Americans. Frank Grippe marked the LZ about 200 metres from the Halfpipe. As the choppers roared in, the men gathered their gear and made for the open tail ramps. High above in the clear night air a AC-130 gunship covered their withdrawal, blasting anything that moved in the ridgelines.

Warrant Officer Clint Palmer and Signaller Jock Wallace travelled on different helicopters on that two-hour journey back to Bagram. Jock was just pleased to be out of danger and heading home. Clint's state of mind was very different as he reviewed the total collapse of Anaconda's D-Day operation and the reactions of the commanders when called upon to adapt to the changed circumstances. It could all have been so different.

He says he recalled the last few days before embarking on Anaconda. He was on duty as liaison officer early in the evening when the shocking news arrived of the first Australian casualty of the war. 1 Squadron's Sergeant Andy Russell was in a long-range patrol vehicle leading a convoy south of Kandahar when they ran over an anti-tank mine. The driver realised Andy was in big trouble, returned and ripped his belt off to tourniquet his mate's leg.

Word reached Palmer as the Australian Liaison Officer in the Tactical Operations Centre that coordinated the rescue response. Only 23 minutes after the call he had two Black Hawk choppers in the air and heading at speed from Kandahar. At the same time, a C-130 with three medics on board left for the scene. It overtook the Black Hawks and the medics parachuted in and tried to stabilise Andy's condition. (One of those guys was a friend, and was killed two weeks later during the attempted rescue of Neil Roberts.) Reports kept coming in that two bags of Hartman's plasma had been pumped into Andy and he seemed to be hanging on. Just over 20 minutes later the helos arrived and transferred him from stretcher to Stokes litter and lifted off immediately.

But soon after he was airborne he developed problems and began to degenerate. Despite everyone's best efforts he died 30 minutes out of Kandahar. Clint, like the rest of the SAS contingent, was deeply shaken by the loss. Andy was one of the regiment's finest.

The next day he helped organise a wooden coffin to be built for his mate's body.(At this stage, there were no coffins in Kandahar – they had to be flown in from Germany.) 'We sent him off,' he wrote in his diary, 'with a bit of pomp and ceremony' – pipers from Princess Patricia's Canadian Light Infantry played as a C-130 flew him out at 1738. The next two days were blank – no activity to be remembered; just blank. Then on the 21st Clint travelled from Kandahar to Bagram to set up for Anaconda.

The major rehearsal for the operation was on 28 February, three days before the operation. He and Jock were among the 1-87 troops heading out of Bagram in the Chinooks. But there was no system to the loading and they sat on the ground for 40 minutes before take-off, flew for 30 minutes, then landed. They disembarked as an undisciplined mob. No one seemed to know where to go or what to do.

That was a clear failure of leadership. And worse – though he raised the issue with the Americans, absolutely nothing was done to correct the problem. Exactly the same thing happened on D-Day. The troops straggled from the aircraft 'in a column of blob', just a mass of people spewing out the back of a CH-47; and then as the first enemy rounds landed 'people scattered in all directions'.

As the helicopter roared through the darkness, with the wounded guys in the centre and the rest scattered round the edges, Palmer says he mentally prepared his report to SAS headquarters. 'It appeared that a formation for movement – and effective leadership – was absent,' he drafted. When the first rounds smashed among them, 'It was very much a case of every man for himself.' By the time they collected into safe areas, the American NCOs who, in the SASR and across the Australian forces kept a tight rein on their men, would do nothing 'until an officer barked directions at them'. And the same thing had just occurred when the Chinooks arrived to extract them.

'It seemed to me that a fundamental problem was the lack of top-to-bottom briefing. On the battlefield it was obvious to me that each soldier was an individual and not part of a well-trained and disciplined team. Fire discipline was mostly regulated by someone screaming, "Stop firing!" Rates of fire, which we instil into our soldiers, appeared to go out the window. Fear and self-preservation took over from any discipline in this regard . . . machine-gun fire was not controlled well. Two general purpose machine guns had run out of ammunition by mid-morning. Ammo was in the packs left out in the open when they came under fire and dropped them.

'Ammunition is the most critical item to carry when on a mission – and obviously there is a limit to what can be carried. With a belt-fed machine gun it is more difficult to carry, as it comes in 100-round linked belts. One belt is on the weapon, and at least two more should be carried by the man on the top of the back pack for easy access. As it turned out in that case, the gunners had only taken the 100-round belts, and all the other ammo was in their packs. When the shooting started, these particular guys dropped their packs immediately – against any of the methods taught to Australians – and were never able to recover them. So they ran out of ammo very soon after opening fire!'

Tactically, the operation was a disaster. That started with the decision to locate the landing zones in the valley floor as opposed to the high ground. The officers had refused to reconsider the issue. 'The planning staff,' Clint decided, 'seeemed more concerned about the distance they had to walk to the blocking point than a tactically sound approach from a different LZ.'

Little scope was given to platoon leaders; and squad leaders in the main were just members within the squad. There appeared to be a considerable gap between company command and the soldier.'

Leadership seemed the big problem. 'Dissemination of info down the line was a major concern. Why did the blue-on-blue occur? The soldiers involved denied any knowledge of friendlies in the area. Officers are taught doctrine and know it well, but this same information is not taught to soldiers in language they can understand. Everything has textbook titles and acronyms that translate to a blank look from soldiers. The whole affair seemed to have a handful of people making some decisions (based on doctrine); everything else was reactive, or "just in time".

In short, it was a shemozzle, and now 30 soldiers were paying for it with wounds and injuries, some of which would torture them for the rest of their lives. As the Chinook made its swift descent into Bagram, he says he could feel the rage clamping his teeth together. When it landed, the pilot lowered the tailgate, and as the medics came aboard to help the wounded, he and the others deplaned. It was nearing 2 a.m. and he headed towards the Australian encampment. Jock grabbed him in a bear hug while someone else ripped the pack off Palmer's back 'Bloody great to see you, mate. Where the fuck did you get to?' Jock said before releasing him.

A small group of officers was waiting and as he approached, Rowan Tink stepped forward. 'He had a big grin on his face,' Palmer says. 'He was smiling, "Hey, welcome home." He went to shake my hand and I didn't shake his hand. I stuck my finger under his chin and I said, "Don't you ever do that to me again."'

Tink responded, 'At least I got you out of there.'

Palmer says, 'I just walked off. I got into a vehicle and went back down to the headquarters, spoke to S3, the operations officer and S2, the intelligence officer, and gave each a 20-minute debrief on how I saw the day.' Palmer claims, the S2 became one of the casualties of the day. 'He melted down after that – came back to Australia, got out of the army and a year or two later had a nervous breakdown, all over that one day . . .'

Palmer reached his bunk and hit the sack. 'I reckon I aged 20 years that day,' he says. 'I was that knackered I went to sleep pretty much straight away.' He woke the following morning seeing the roof above him swaying from side to side. 'I jumped up and ran outside the hangar where the whole HQ were already standing. When they saw me they yelled, "Get out quick" – there was an earthquake which measured 7.2 on the Richter scale, and all personnel from both HQs were outside – except me! I was not happy that no one had woken me but then I realised I was tucked away in a corner so as not to be disturbed, and therefore couldn't be found quickly. The next few days I spent liaising with people trying to secure some real estate so the task force could move out of the hangar.'

After the disastrous opening gambit, the American command recalibrated their approach to Operation Anaconda, and over the next two weeks they poured a massive airborne and ground assault into the Shahi-Kot Valley. When the dust cleared, the Americans judged themselves to be successful. As proof they offered a series of wildly differing enemy body counts. No high-value targets from the al-Qaeda leadership were forthcoming. However, Lieutenant Colonel LaCamera had returned to the fray and in due course was awarded the Silver Star and given command of his own Ranger battalion.

'Funnily enough,' Palmer says, 'years later when I'm in Baghdad I ran into Frank Grippe and his demeanour on the whole thing seemed to be different. By now LaCamara was gone; he didn't have to worry about his loyalty to the individual. That was history. He'd done the right thing at the time. The American glue stuck fast. But he was quite candid with me about it.'

However, in the days that followed his confrontation with his task force commander on the Bagram airstrip, he realised it had been a bad career move. He was not asked to participate in the secondary phase of Anaconda. And the true extent of his fall from grace was driven home several weeks later when Jock Wallace was awarded the Medal for Gallantry. It would be presented by the Governor-General, Peter Hollingworth, at Yarralumla on 27 November 2002. Three other SAS soldiers (a corporal, a sergeant and a captain) also received awards anonymously for their involvement in Anaconda. The regiment's commanding officer, (then Lieutenant Colonel Gus Gilmore), was awarded the Distinguished Service Cross.

Palmer was ignored. And it hurt.

It would also have a devastating, if indirect, effect on his family life.

If only . . . It is a theme that recurs several times in the career and personal progress of one of the SAS's longest serving and most polarising figures. It is an essential ingredient in a long and improbable passage. It is a measure of the man that time and again he would overcome setbacks that would have felled a lesser being. And in this he and his journey reflect in so many ways the fighting unit that dominated his life and times: the Australian Special Air Services Regiment (SASR).

4

TOUGH SPEARHEAD

The SAS had its genesis in the sands of North Africa in the early years of World War II. And its instigator and guiding light, Lieutenant David Stirling, was a figure who, like Palmer, attracted more than his share of controversy. However, the family and social backgrounds of the two men could hardly have been more different.

Clint Palmer, as we shall see, was born in the most humble circumstances in a gimcrack mining settlement in the untamed isolation of Australia's Northern Territory. Stirling, the son of a British Army general with aristocratic connections, came from the *crème de la crème* of County society. He took for granted his life of privilege, attended Cambridge until sent down for gambling, dabbled in art in Paris until his lack of talent found him out; conceived an obsession to be the first man to climb Mount Everest but was thwarted in this unlikely quest by the outbreak of war.

He used his social connections to secure selection in a venture sponsored by Winston Churchill in the aftermath of Dunkirk to develop a brigade of commandos to harrass the Germans behind the lines. It was commanded by a fellow White's Club member, Colonel Bob Laycock of the Royal Horse Guards. However, after a series of disastrous interventions in Crete and Syria, 'Layforce', as it was known, fetched up in Cairo. Having lost half its fighting strength it was judged to be no longer a viable unit.

Just before Layforce was disbanded, Stirling's colleague Jock Lewes spotted some parachutes left behind on the wharf and asked the commander if they could be used to teach some of the chaps to jump. Stirling was one of four to take the leap into the unknown. 'I was a bit unlucky,' he says. 'We had tied our static cords and parachutes to the legs of the seats and when I jumped I must have gone horizontal to the slipstream, because when it opened my chute was attached to the tailplane and it tore an enormous number of panels away.'[4]

'Luckily it opened as a parachute but obviously let a lot more air through, so I descended a great deal faster than my companions. I hit the ground very, very hard and really put a crater in the desert. I was paralysed and they had to take me to hospital.'

It was during his forced lay-up over the next three weeks that Stirling conceived and outlined on paper his idea for a Special Force, acting independently in small teams that would parachute at night behind enemy lines, commit acts of sabotage then return secretly to base. 'I was still on crutches when I went to Middle East HQ with my plan,' Stirling says. 'I didn't tell anyone [in the lower ranks] who might have spoilt my surprise. They were layer upon layer of fossilised shit. I had to get to the generals like Ritchie [deputy chief of general staff] and Auchinleck [commander-in-chief].'

In Stirling's account, when he was refused entry to GHQ he used his crutches to vault over the wire. He then staggered into the office of Neil Ritchie, who had shot grouse with Stirling's father. Ritchie agreed to read the paper. 'When he finished, Ritchie said he would submit it right away to Auchinleck ... meantime I should get going preparing a camp and recruiting 65 men from Layforce.' And while Stirling was inclined to overdramatise his activities, the bones of his account are verified by British military records.

He used all sorts of unconventional methods to secure his men and equipment – including outright theft from a New Zealand contingent – and even adopted the name Special Air Services (SAS) to gain the cooperation of Colonel Dudley Clark, who had been using it in one of his schemes to confuse the Germans about the strength and disposition of Allied forces by releasing dummy parachutes in unexpected locations.

However, his first and most significant recruit was John Steel 'Jock' Lewes, an Oxford graduate who had spent his childhood in Australia. For while Stirling would provide the inspiration, Lewes would be responsible for the organisation, the training and the tactical expertise to run the show. On their first mission – on 17 November 1941 – his team set out from Kabrit airfield to parachute behind German lines on the coastal strip west of Tobruk. There they would use Lewes's patent incendiary devices to destroy scores of Messerschmitt BF-109, parked beside their runways.

Unfortunately, a ferocious gale blew up and Stirling was faced with the possibility of postponing the operation. 'I swore when I started the SAS that if we undertook to take on a target on a particular night, we'd do it utterly regardless,' he says. 'I simply wasn't prepared to see the first of our operations being postponed because of bad weather.'5

It was a disastrous decision. Of the 54 men who took off in five ancient Bombay aircraft that night, only 21 returned. Those who jumped landed in 70 kilometre-an-hour winds that dragged them across the desert and flayed them alive with jagged rocks and needle-sharp deadwood that covered the drop zones. Stirling says, 'My stick came down about 12 miles [17 kilometres] from where it ought to have been. And it was a night without any moon, pitch-black. When we hit the ground quite a few of us were knocked out and it was a struggle to get out of one's parachute rigging.'

Those who landed safely had to search a trackless waste for the 'Lewes bombs', weaponry, water and food that had been dropped separately. One stick was captured by an Italian patrol; another floated out to sea and all were drowned. One group didn't jump at all. Their aircraft was hit by flak and later shot down by a Messerschmitt BF-109. The survivors were rounded up by German troops.

Those who avoided death, serious injury or capture were rescued by the Long Range Desert Group – drawn initially from New Zealand forces – who had proved themselves expert at eluding Rommel's troops during extended reconnaissance missions. Each patrol, travelling in specially modified trucks, incorporated a medical orderly, a navigator, a radio operator and a vehicle mechanic. Their arrival was doubly valuable since, according to Stirling's founding SAS colleague Reg Seekings, 'Everybody said: "Well, crikey, if these people can penetrate this far, why the hell take all the risk and trouble [of] a parachute drop. Why not get them to carry us in?" It was so obvious. We had no idea that we had patrols penetrating two, three, or four hundred miles behind the enemy position. And so we quickly adopted that method.'[6]

However, Stirling knew that if he reported his initial fiasco to MEHQ immediately, the 'fossilised shits' in the military's middle management would blow his SAS away in a blizzard of snotty memoranda. So he simply returned to his Kabrit base camp and said nothing. Three days later he learned of an operation commanded by Brigadier Denys Reid to send a flying column across the desert to hit Rommel's forces from the south. The LRDG was involved and its commander, Lieutenant Colonel Guy Prendergast, was an old pal from White's.

Prendergast signalled HQ with a suggestion that 'parachutists [be] used for blowing dromes'. And when approval was granted, Stirling and his men were back in business.

Stirling contacted Lewes, who rounded up the survivors, and two days later they assembled at Brigadier Reid's HQ. The LRDG took them out into the desert, and in a series of raids on enemy airfields they destroyed aircraft, munitions, fuel installations and vital road systems. 'The successes gave [us] enormous self-confidence and a feeling of exhilaration which I very much shared myself', Stirling says. 'And of course it led to great puzzlement in Middle East Headquarters because they had lost track of us. They'd forgotten about us in effect and they didn't know who the hell was destroying these aircraft up front. It was only when they got a dispatch from the 8th Army they realised [we] would be coming back for recruiting and a considerable expansion of establishment. That of course hit them rather hard. But it made us feel rather happy.'

Stirling was awarded the DSO and promoted to major. The one desperately sad note from the operation was the death of Jock Lewes, who was killed in action in December

1941. He was returning from a raid on German airfields when the LRDG truck he was travelling in was attacked by a lone Messerschmitt Bf 110 fighter. Lewes was fatally wounded in the thigh by a 20-millimetre round and bled to death in about four minutes. He was buried on the site and the whereabouts of his grave is today unknown. David Stirling says, 'Jock could far more genuinely claim to be founder of the SAS than I.'[7]

It was Stirling who directed the subsequent development of the unit. Although he was captured by the Germans in January 1943 and spent the rest of the war in various POW camps (having escaped four times), his independent, hard-hitting, bend-the-rules influence remains at the heart of Special Forces operations. His SAS was disbanded in 1945 but re-established briefly during the Korean conflict and found its modern incarnation as 22 SAS Regiment during the Malaya Emergency in the 1950s. It was during this time that its Australian equivalent came into being.

The British SAS in Malaya was under the command of Brigadier Mike Calvert and was scoring notable successes against the communist insurgents. By chance, a Cambridge graduate, Stewart Harris, who had served as an SAS operator under Calvert in 1951 then migrated to Australia and was appointed editorial writer at the Brisbane *Courier-Mail*. He retained strong links with the Special Forces and military community both in the UK and Australia and became a leading advocate for the creation of an Australian SAS. By 1957 he had been appointed the *Times* correspondent in Australia and relocated to Canberra, where he continued his agitation at the heart of the military establishment.

He remained in this journalistic role in the early 1960s and was close to the Canberra Bureau of the *Age*, headed by John Bennetts, a former intelligence operator in World War II. Bennetts later became an analyst at the Defence Department's Joint Intelligence Organisation. Harris was encouraged by the British SAS leadership as well as the Australian Governor-General, Sir William Slim (1953–59) and his son John Slim, who had served in the British SAS in Malaya.[8] While the intricacies of the official military and political record remain clouded, on 4 April 1957 the Menzies Government's Minister for the Army John Cramer announced the formation of the SAS.

At Defence HQ in Canberra there was an intense period of organisation and establishment for the new unit. Its recruits – volunteers from all army corps – were to be aged between 18 and 35, be from 5 foot 3 inches (160 centimetres) to 6 foot 1 inch (185 centimetres), weighing no more than 13 stone (82.6 kilograms), with a reasonable standard of education, undoubted medical fitness and a higher level of aptitude than ordinary soldiers. And they had to be trained parachutists 'or volunteers for such training'.[9]

Minister Cramer said they would be chosen for their 'rugged individuality' and would be a 'tough spearhead to penetrate enemy territory'. On long-range reconnaissance missions they could be dropped behind the lines to carry out specified tasks before withdrawing. They would be among Australia's most highly trained fighting men, he said, and would include specialists in demolitions, cliff climbing and small craft handling.

The volunteers were quickly forthcoming and included at least one seasoned soldier, Ray Simpson, who would subsequently win the Victoria Cross. The unit – at company strength – formally began operations on 1 September 1957. Its transitional commanding officer Major William 'Wally' Cook took the salute at its designated headquarters – Campbell Barracks, Swanbourne, a Perth suburb fronting the Indian Ocean. By the time his permanent replacement Major Len Eyles took command on 1 February 1958, 1 SAS Company was at reasonable strength and fully operational.

Eyles was a first-rate choice as the founding CO. A down-to-earth character, he was born in Parramatta in 1926, graduated from Duntroon Military College in 1947 and fought in Korea, where he was mentioned in dispatches in the pivotal Battle of Kapyong. He then distinguished himself in a series of infantry postings before joining the School of Land/Air Warfare at Williamtown. On completion he was posted to Britain for advanced training as a parachute jumping instructor. He returned to Williamtown as a senior army instructor in 1956.

On arrival at Campbell Barracks he immediately instituted a vigorous training regime, and in October 1958 he spent two weeks in Malaya observing his British counterparts in action. This convinced him that Australia's elite Special Forces unit should develop its own *modus operandi* rather than copy its imperial forebear. For while jungle operations might well form an important element of its future operations, its first priority was the defence of the homeland. And that meant he and his men must become expert in all the survival and operational skills demanded by Australia's unique conditions and terrain.

He was also determined to create a powerful sense of *esprit de corps*. It would draw on the swashbuckling traditions of David Stirling and his 'originals', but the real and lasting foundations would have to be home grown. And they would begin with extraordinarily long-range reconnaissance operations from Perth to Darwin and over the trackless waste of northern Western Australia in the most testing conditions for men and machines. At the same time, he sent all his officers and men in select groups to Williamtown, where they underwent intensive parachute training. By 1959 they were conducting mass jumps in WA and these would become an annual public attraction at different drop zones (DZs) in the state's south-west corner.

During one exercise in the Kimberleys in February 1960, two members of the company had to abandon a 12-foot rubber dinghy when a saltwater crocodile climbed aboard in deep water at Montague Sound. Sharks were known to frequent the area, but the two men remained with the craft, gingerly pulled up the anchor and towed the dinghy to shore with the massive reptile aboard. Fortunately when they reached the shallows the crocodile departed to seaward. Private John Sexton and his superior officer Mike Jeffrey breathed a sigh of relief. Lieutenant Jeffrey would rise through the ranks to become Australia's Governor-General (2003–08).

By 1960 the company had reached its full complement of 12 officers and 182 other ranks. The CO had welded them into a solid aggressive unit with specialist skills in vehicle-mounted reconnaissance operations. However, with growing destabilisation in South-East Asia – notably in President Sukarno's Indonesia and Ho Chi Minh's anti-colonialist operations in French Indo-China – it was necessary to reorient training to include infantry patrolling in tropical conditions.

The change of emphasis coincided with the arrival of Len Eyles' successor, Major Lawrie Clark, who, like his predecessor, had graduated from Duntroon in 1947 and served with distinction in Korea, where he earned the Military Cross. His subsequent postings had taken him to the United States, where he was able to observe the Special Forces and the Ranger battalions (the equivalent of the British commandos) in training. He liked what he saw, particularly the concept of 'pushing people beyond their perceived limits'. This led him to introduce the signature 'selection' courses that came to define the elite nature of the Australian SAS.

Clark also reorganised the training regime and established a special platoon to conduct courses in roping, driving, small-scale amphibious raids, small craft handling and close-order combat. The results were tested in 'recondo' (reconnaissance/ commando) operations for up to 20 days and both troopers and officers were required to pass the course to remain in the unit.

The company expanded its training operations to South-East Asia and in 1962 joined a major SEATO exercise in Thailand. At the same time the government announced a commitment of 30 army instructors to the South Vietnamese forces. These included four NCOs from the SAS and one of them, Ray Simpson, would win the VC.

More significantly perhaps, the OC, Lawrie Clark was also included and during his absence his 2IC, Captain Geoff Cohen, took charge.

Involvement in the South-East Asian conflicts would mark a turning point in the unit's history. But before the SAS deployed as an operational force, it would be fully reorganised and raised to regimental status. Major-General J. S. Anderson, commander of the 1st Division, took the salute as the SAS Regiment was formally inaugurated in a parade at Campbell

Barracks on 4 September 1964. Its originals had been training for more than seven years without ever coming to grips with a hostile force. Its 15 officers and 209 other ranks were now ready and anxious to prove themselves in the only arena that counted in the soldier's lexicon: the battlefield.

5

THE EARLY YEARS

When the SAS was formed in March 1957, Clint Palmer was just seven weeks old, having come into the world in far-off Batchelor, 90 kilometres from Darwin, on 21 February, the third in a family of seven children, each one of whom would subsequently join the Australian Defence Force. By the time the unit had achieved regimental status he was a seven-year-old adventurer, living an idyllic childhood in the bush and rockpools of Rum Jungle and the Finness River.

'As a boy, all I ever knew was the footloose, carefree existence of a small town, with no crime and where everyone knew each other,' he says. He had a readymade 'gang' with his elder brothers Garry and Blake and the younger Dean, together with a couple of mates from school. 'We built bikes from any spare parts we could find at the dump and we rode everywhere,' he says. 'We went to the original Rum Jungle and fished in the creek. We made race tracks in the red soil and rode though the bush chasing wallabies.'

But the really outstanding times were spent at Meneling Station where he and his brothers would link up with Kathy, Margy, Richard and Linda Daiyi, the Aboriginal family of local cattleman Max Sargent, one of the Territory's larger-than-life 'characters'. Invariably they were led on their expeditions by the Aboriginal kids' mother, Nancy.

'She was a wonderful person,' Palmer says. 'She was the leader. She taught us everything about bushcraft. She brought the place alive. We would walk for miles following the tracks of goannas, pigs and echidnas. When we found fresh tracks, we would follow up and find the hidey hole and dig them out. Some we would kill and cook up out there, some we would take back for the old [Aboriginal] people at the station.'

Max Sargent divided his time between his Aboriginal family and his European wife, Ada, and their daughter Roslyn, who lived in the homestead while Nancy and the kids lived in a handmade tin house next door. 'In the afternoons, Nancy was always waiting in the Toyota parked under a tree near the school,' Clint says. 'Max was usually at the pub. He was a bit of a rogue, but Nancy was just great. She was like a second mother to us.'

His 'first' mother, Isabel (Bonnie), was a highly skilled dressmaker and cared for the growing Palmer family in their home on stilts in the Batchelor township. She came from Brisbane, where her father was a school bus driver who ran pigs on a small property on the suburban outskirts. Clint's father, Terry, had been born at Blackall, son of a railway fettler, and during World War II, he and his brothers had been placed in the Salvation Army boys' home at Indooroopilly. 'Mum's dad picked the kids up from the home in the bus and dropped them at school each day,' Clint says. 'And that's how they met.'

They would marry in Ann Street Presbyterian Church, Brisbane on 23 December 1950. Terry had joined the army in 1948 and after serving nearly six years decided to leave and make a life in civvy street. He applied for a job in the administration section of the Rum Jungle mine, where they extracted and processed uranium for the Australian Atomic Energy Commission. He was still a serving member but would be available on his discharge early in 1954. He was successful and they arrived in Batchelor with their eldest son Garry, who had been born in Brisbane in 1952.

The mine was operated by Territory Enterprises, a subsidiary of ConZinc Rio Tinto Australia (CRA). It built the town for a population of about 600 but during the peak mining period of the late 1950s and early 1960s that number was regularly exceeded. Batchelor's airfield had been built in 1933 and substantially upgraded during World War II as a major base for both the Australian and United States air forces. By the 1960s there were two adjoining strips: one dirt, the other sealed and almost 3 kilometres long. The airport had returned to its civilian status and attracted the Darwin Parachute Club, who arrived most weekends to jump from about 10,000 feet and land – hopefully – on the adjoining flat. When they weren't out with the gang, Clint and Blake would walk over to the airfield, lie on their backs and watch the jumpers – in sticks of three or four – floating down towards them.

'When they'd lose bits and pieces – ripcords and spring-loaded pilot chutes, etc – we'd go around the bush until we found them,' Clint says. 'They'd give us something for our trouble – maybe a model car or an ice-cream.' And when the club members had wrapped up for the day, Clint and his brothers at home would make their own 'parachutes'. 'We tried to make a really big one out of a clothes line and an old sheet. I had about eight strings on it . . . never worked, of course. But at least no one got badly hurt.'

The Batchelor idyll came to a temporary halt in 1965 when Terry decided to take the family back to Brisbane. However, although he had completed a bookkeeping course, his qualifications limited the opportunities available in the city and they returned about 18 months later.

'We fitted back in like we'd never left,' Palmer says. He and his father and brothers all played hockey for the local team and the boys resumed their bush expeditions with the Daiyi/Sargent family. However, by 1970 the Rum Jungle mine was coming to the end of its natural life and was heading for a phased close-down in 1974. 'People were starting to leave,' Clint says, 'and Dad took an administrative job at the Mammoth mine at a place called Gunpowder just north-east of Mount Isa.' There they mined copper but when commodity prices collapsed they closed the mine and Terry was out of a job. Fortunately, Terry had maintained his contacts and he was able to apply for a job in another of CRA's Australian operations. They responded with an offer of a position in far-off Kalgoorlie. 'There really wasn't much choice,' he says, 'so we packed up and headed off.'

The move itself was a major logistical operation. By now Garry, Blake, Clint and Dean had been joined by Kirk in 1960, Nita in 1961 and Brenda in 1963. 'Mum and the girls and the two young boys flew to Brisbane; Dad and my two older brothers and I headed off to Alice Springs in the HR Holden sedan, getting there about a week later,' he says. 'We then took the train to Port Augusta via Marree and from there across to Kalgoorlie.'

They arrived at night on 21 February 1971, Clint's fourteenth birthday. 'We got off the train and carried our bags up the street to the Palace Hotel,' he says. 'We booked in, went upstairs, and it was freezing. I'd never been this far south before.' The company put them up at the hotel for several weeks until a house became available. 'Mum and the girls joined us and we moved into a little company house in Killarney Street. It was tiny – three bedrooms, one bathroom – and Mum said, "Oh, I can't do this", and Dad went to the boss who told him to put an extension on the back. So it became a five and two – three in the house and two bedrooms and a bathroom in the back extension. It was better after that.'

School had started a week before their arrival and this would prove a real problem. 'I started high school in Batchelor, as the school was a Higher Primary and catered for kids up to Year 10,' Clint says. 'But when we went to Gunpowder there was no high school so I repeated 7th Grade.' The Queensland curriculum was very different from the Territory's and now he faced yet another curriculum in WA at the Eastern Goldfields Senior High School. So by the time he reached Kalgoorlie he was a full year behind his cohort.

He also experienced some learning difficulties. 'I never found reading interesting,' he says. 'My father used to read to us and I was mesmerised; I enjoy Australiana and he used to read Banjo Paterson, all sorts of stuff, but I've never gotten into reading myself.' Moreover, he didn't mix easily in the new environment. 'The first day I was at school, I was sitting eating my lunch and this kid came over and took one of my sandwiches. I just got up and thumped him, bang, and down he went. He didn't do that again.

'I don't classify myself as a loner but I do prefer my own company and school was no different. I couldn't handle certain types of people. I just picked people who I got on with and spent time with them. I did like girls, though, and soon made friends with many of the girls in my year. I kept a small group of people from that time as long-term friends – and I maintain contact with most of them today.'

His first love was sport, all sorts of team games, particularly hockey, basketball and Aussie Rules football; cricket less so. 'I played one or two games of cricket and gave it away,' he says. 'My timetable was full with basketball anyway.' Their home backed on to the Kalgoorlie Golf Course and Clint spent hours on the range and down the rough fairways with a mate during the sweltering summer holidays mastering the game's basics.

Sport helped a lot in settling into the life of Kalgoorlie, with its own unique ethos of isolated frontier mining town. Prospector Paddy Hannan had famously discovered gold there in 1893 and at its height the subsequent gold rush brought more than 200,000 eager prospectors to the area. It quickly gained a reputation as a law unto itself, with conmen, gamblers and prostitutes abounding, most notoriously in its two-up school and its Hay Street brothels.

By the 1970s it had become a prosperous settled community of about 30,000. However, the Hay Street establishments remained, and when the Palmer family outgrew its initial home the company found them a bigger one in Hay Street itself, some little distance from the garish bordellos. Clint walked past them each day on his way home from high school. 'The girls would be outside and they'd say, "Hello, how are you doing, young man?" I'd stop and say, "Good day" and check them out. I was a 15, 16-year-old kid. They'd want to know where I lived and "Does your dad work in the mines? What about your mum?"

"Oh no, she's home."

"And what does she do?"

"Nothing, she's at home just busy dressmaking."

"Oh, she's a dressmaker, is she?"

"Yeah, that's right."

"Oh, okay. Well, do you think she'd make dresses for me?"

"I don't know, why don't you ask her?"

"Okay, what's your phone number?"

'So word got out and the girls started coming down to the house. Of course, mum didn't discriminate and they were willing to pay good money for the work. I found it quite amusing because I knew that in one way I was responsible for it. But I used to enjoy coming home from school when they were there because they all had expensive cars and I would see the Jags parked out the front. I always knew when they'd been there,' he laughs, 'I could smell their perfume even before I got in the front door. She'd be up late many, many nights. She had two treadle sewing machines and then she got the press-button job. She actually had a flash Janome by the time she'd finished.'

The second big innovation at high school was the Army Cadet Corps, and Clint signed up at 15, the first possible opportunity. 'I just took to cadets,' he says. 'Something about the order, the clarity, the proper way to operate and handle things; I just felt it was for me. I was serious about it right from the beginning. I had that bush background, and the outdoors was also part of who I am so I looked forward to the activities that cadets offered. The army stuff – marching and drill – was something you just had to do, but the weapon handling was a boy thing and I'd had plenty of experience with rifles up at Meneling Station. My final year in cadets left me wondering if a career in the military beckoned, but I wasn't sure until Captain Barry Corse persuaded me to apply for officer training.'

Though he didn't know it, Clint had taken the first step in a military career that would take him to the top echelon of Australia's elite Special Forces. But he would arrive by an extraordinarily roundabout route; and with more brutal ups and downs than a Punch and Judy show.

•

By 1971, the SASR had come to a crossroads in establishing its own maturing persona. In the mid-60s, there had been a move to integrate the regiment with the 'big army' units but its leadership had successfully opposed the move. One leader of the resistance was Major Alf Garland in his role as OC of 1 SAS Squadron. And when some of his men were attached to the British 22 SAS Regiment on operations against the Indonesians early in 1965, he quickly realised that the two forces had differing approaches to their tasks. For example, the British tactic of 'shoot and scoot' involved their leaving wounded comrades behind in direct contrast to the Australian (and American) military ethos. So when the Australian Government committed the SASR to the conflict in Borneo it was as a totally self-contained Australian unit.

Nevertheless, 1 Squadron operated within the overall British command of actions against Indonesian incursions into Sarawak, and its first patrols were deployed in March 1965 in a 'hearts and minds' operation in Brunei. By May they were conducting limited cross-border patrols into Indonesian Kalimantan in four-man teams from both Sarawak and Sabah. By 8 June they had conducted 11 reconnaissance patrols observing enemy activity, but without firing a shot in anger. Their one contact with an aggressor was totally unexpected. On 2 June two a patrol was attacked by a wild elephant, and despite their peppering it with no fewer than nine rifle shots, it gored and mortally wounded one member, Lance

Corporal Paul Denehey, who died in the jungle four days later despite desperate attempts by his patrol to extract him.

Later that month, they accompanied a unit of Gurkhas into Indonesian territory, engaged in a brief firefight and escaped without casualties. They also attempted to ambush an Indonesian patrol, having first laid Claymore mines, but they failed to explode and the action was abandoned. They finally achieved their first enemy 'kills' on 3 July when a patrol opened fire on a boat on Kalimantan's Salilir River. According to the patrol leader Sergeant John Petit, it carried nine men – eight paddled and the ninth, 'wearing an olive green shirt and trousers and a green cloth cap'[10] appeared to be in command. As it approached within 10 metres of Petit's position he opened fire and 'in less than a minute his patrol poured 81 rounds of [rifle fire] and 26 rounds of Owen gun into the boat'. There was no return fire. Petit reported that he had killed seven and seriously wounded two. Two days later, another patrol took out two Indonesian soldiers before moving quickly back into the jungle, while several other patrols on the Salilir recorded several more kills.

Garland mounted several larger-scale operations but they were either cancelled at the last minute or failed to make contact with the enemy. The squadron ended its tour on 2 August and was withdrawn soon after. Its Borneo operations remained secret for the next 20 years.

However, later that year the regiment took another step in its development with a change of uniform, from the red to a sand-coloured beret with a metal badge depicting the Flaming Sword Excalibur and the motto adopted by David Stirling, 'Who dares wins'. They also added a blue lanyard with black Sam Browne belts for officers and warrant officers. All ranks who were parachute qualified wore the SAS paratroop wings.

The commanding officer, Major Bill Braithwaite, 44, had been appointed in August 1964. He had distinguished himself in Z Special unit operating behind the lines in Borneo during World War II and after the war he had served with the SEATO military secretariat in Bangkok, so was well versed in the regiment's areas of special interest. He authorised and oversaw further squadron patrolling in the Indonesian 'confrontation' during 1966, but by then, following an attempted communist coup and the rise of General Suharto, Sukarno was becoming a spent force and a new era would soon commence in Australian–Indonesian relations.

The government's attention was now focused on Vietnam, and on 8 March 1966 Prime Minister Harold Holt announced Australia's commitment to that conflict would be increased from 1,400 to a self-contained task force of 4,500, including 3 SAS Squadron with various support units. Braithwaite planned for the squadron to complete its training and preparation by 8 June. Then for the first time the regiment would be blooded in a major war. The SAS would operate in Phuoc Tuy Province, some 70 kilometres south-east of Saigon, for the next five years. The experience and its effect on the SAS and its traditions would be pivotal, but by no means without its drawbacks.

6

TRAINING

Three Squadron conducted their final training for Vietnam in Papua New Guinea in May 1966 and arrived in Saigon on 15 June. They moved on to their HQ at Nui Dat on the Phuoc Tuy coast a few days later. The commander, Major John Murphy, who had fought in Korea, successfully resisted attempts to incorporate elements of the squadron into the task force infantry battalions, 5 and 6 RAR. He then began a series of independent patrols searching for Viet Cong main forces and providing early warning of movements to the battalion commanders.

This intelligence became tremendously valuable to the task force commanders and the SAS developed a close working relationship with the men of 9 Squadron RAAF, who frequently extracted them under fire from the Viet

Cong. However, they had been in the country for only two months when the soldiers of D Company 6 RAR engaged enemy forces in the Battle of Long Tan on 18 August, the biggest single Australian combat engagement of the war. The squadron had failed to warn them of the build-up surrounding the Australians, and this still rankles with some SAS veterans. From time to time suggestions have been made that they did inform task force HQ only to have their warnings ignored, but there is no published evidence to support the contention. Nevertheless, the relationship with 6 RAR, its officers and men, remained strong, and SAS patrols constantly operated in advance of the battalion, providing vital intelligence on the enemy's disposition.

3 Squadron had ended its tour in February and was replaced the following month by 1 Squadron, led by Major Dale Burnett, a 30-year-old Duntroon graduate, who had served in Malaya with the infantry. He had undergone six months' commando training with the Rangers at the United States Infantry School in Fort Benning, Georgia, and was then appointed adjutant and quartermaster of the Sydney Commando Company. This was followed by a posting to the Officer Cadet School at Portsea.

Once established in Vietnam, Burnett proved to be a highly competent leader. 1 Squadron continued the work of its predecessor and added to its combat repertoire with a series of short, sharp ambushes. They also attempted to capture Viet Cong soldiers for interrogation, but without notable success. The squadron's tour was extended to nine months in the field, an absurdly long period for Special Forces soldiers to be exposed to the unremitting stresses of the battlefield. Moreover, many of the 1 Squadron men had struggled through the exhausting jungle conditions of Borneo the year before. But as in all previous (and subsequent) conflicts, the military and political taskmasters seemed to have no real conception of the psychological and physical damage inherent in extended combat stress. Once again, the men at the front would pay.

Increasingly the Vietnam War threw the SAS and the United States Special Forces together in the most challenging conditions. This gradually led to a sense of mutual camaraderie, and relationships developed at both the professional and personal levels. And since Britain was not involved in the conflict, Australia's SAS became steadily more oriented towards the American model. At the same time, the SAS soldiers developed a mystique among their military compatriots as the ultimate in the warrior breed. Their behind-the-lines operations and their refusal to share their experiences and techniques with outsiders contributed an air of exclusivity and even glamour to the SASR.

Through the years that followed, the SAS in Vietnam added an increasingly aggressive role to its reconnaissance operations. The task force commander from October 1967,

Brigadier Ron Hughes, says he saw the SAS 'primarily as a means of harassing the enemy in his base areas or on his routes to and from his source of supply. I did not view the SAS as an intelligence gathering organisation, rather as a reaction force to intelligence gathered by other means. The kill rate achieved by the SAS was very gratifying.'[11]

1 Squadron gave way to 2 Squadron in February 1968, and thereafter the units rotated as required. Commander Hughes's replacement in October 1968, Brigadier Sandy Pearson, was less impressed. 'Some of their actions appeared to be successful,' he wrote later. 'They provided information and contributed greatly to harassment and attrition. But we were never successful in contacting enemy based on that information . . . The time [SAS patrols] spent on the ground between insertion and extraction got progressively shorter. In fact, they were requesting almost immediate extraction – in some cases minutes only – which made the whole operation farcical and expensive in helicopter hours.'[12]

This attitude only added to the operational stresses endured over long periods in the field. Squadron commander at the time Major Brian Wade regarded Pearson's comments as 'an injustice' to the SASR. And indeed, Pearson was known to have opposed the SAS's independence from the 'big army' well before they arrived in Vietnam.

Back at Swanbourne, Lieutenant Colonel Len Eyles had returned as commanding officer and set about improving selection, training and accommodation facilities at Campbell Barracks. Now the new SAS trooper would be taught navigation, contact drills, tracking, unarmed combat, driving, free-fall parachuting, small craft handling, extended underwater diving, canoeing, cliff climbing and helicopter rope drills (rappelling). Special attention was given to the medic course, with five weeks at the School of Army Health in Victoria followed by a month attached to a hospital in WA. The signals course had an even higher priority, including an intense six weeks' instruction in receiving and sending Morse code.

In 1970 and 1971, the tempo of the war in Phuoc Tuy Province decreased markedly and the SAS patrols were frustratingly restricted to areas relatively close to the task force base. However, when a new TF commander, Brigadier Bill Henderson, arrived he called the entire squadron together. 'I wanted [extended] reconnaissance and surveillance which would lead to improved intelligence on which to deploy units of the task force,' he says. 'The squadron got the message and from that time onwards we received greater benefit from their operations. We were able to target companies and battalions against enemy concentrations instead of having "hit and run" actions against small enemy groups.'[13]

In Phuoc Tuy they now concentrated on the north-west of the province, but were occasionally involved in deadly contacts closer to base. The last operational patrol concluded on 2 October 1971 without making contact with enemy forces. The final task force commander, Brigadier Bruce McDonald, says, 'The role of the SAS in [intelligence] collection was of dominant importance. I could rely on the accuracy of their reports.' Major Geoff Chipman, who had been 2IC of 3 Squadron in 1966 and commander of 2 Squadron in the final days of the war, says, 'The SAS in Vietnam have at all times been a most valuable asset for any [task force] commander.'[14]

The SAS had established itself as an elite and highly respected force in the battlefield over six years of continuous combat experience in Borneo and Vietnam. However, the extended calm that followed the combat storm would arguably present an even greater challenge to the officers and men to whom peacetime soldiering was contradiction in terms. And no one would become more conscious of the frustrations inherent in the oxymoron than the conscientious young Cadet Under Officer from Kalgoorlie, Clint Palmer.

He had been quickly promoted to sergeant in the Eastern Goldfields Senior High School Cadet Unit, then topped the under officer's course while still in Year 11. The following year he was appointed brigade cadet under officer, the senior CUO in Western Australia. He attended a series of cadet camps at Northam army base, about 100 kilometres north-east of Perth, usually travelling by train from Kalgoorlie. 'One time we drove home in a truck – eight hours in the back;

it was torture – but the camps were great,' he says. 'We'd do navigation courses and learn how to fire weapons, from rifles to Bren guns to mortars. I was very serious about it.'

He attracted the attention of a Vietnam veteran, Captain Barry Corse. 'He was an imposing figure,' Clint says, 'a big guy, deep voice, dressed well, smoked cigars and carried a cane. He was part of the regular army staff attached to the cadet brigade. He supervised all the courses in the camp. I chose him as a mentor. Basically I wanted to be like him. He gave me advice and opportunity. We just went on from there.'

When he left school in 1975, Clint joined most of his schoolmates as an underground miner but at the same time he applied for the Officer Training School in Portsea, Victoria. He was accepted. 'It was fortuitous because I'd decided that I'd had enough of working underground,' he says. 'So I came out of the hole and said, "I'm out of here."'

He left the family to take on a career in the armed services, with his mother Isabel shedding tears of pride. However, he quickly discovered the gap between the cadets and the real army, where officers are expected to maintain high academic standards. 'I was doing well at the military arts and the military skills,' he says. 'It was on the academic side that I let myself down.'

His early learning difficulties now rebounded on him. 'I'm not a good scholar,' he says. 'I didn't have the discipline to study and to apply myself where I needed to and I failed the All Arms exam – not by much, a couple of marks, but I was under the line, so, "See you later." The chief instructor at Portsea at the time was Lieutenant Colonel Blakely, who advised me that I had two options: soldier on at one of the infantry battalions or discharge. In my emotional state I opted for the latter. It was another example of an immature mind reacting on impulse rather than considering carefully the alternative. I faced the boss about 10 a.m., and by 6 p.m. I was on a plane to Perth. It was then that I realised the magnitude of my decision.'

It was a fierce blow to his self-esteem, and he quailed at the thought of facing his mother. 'It was embarrassing going away and then failing,' he says. 'My mother was devastated. I wasn't able to look her in the eye. She had talked about me to all her friends, and I came home a failure. I didn't like that feeling at all. It was a horrible feeling. But at the same time, I understood what my shortfalls were and I knew why I failed and I thought, "Well, I'll think about what I'm going to do." I even talked to two of my mates about going to Rhodesia – they left, but I stayed.

'I went back to the mines and I worked laying pipelines, just labouring, and three months later I decided to join up again. My application was accepted and off I went, this time as a private soldier.'

By then both Garry and Blake had joined the army, and Garry had been cashiered during basic training and left the army prematurely. Blake had joined in 1973 and was in the engineering corps. But unlike his younger brother, Blake had no special desire for promotion. Even at that early stage, Clint had an underlying ambition: to join the SAS.

'When I was 15 at Northam doing my sergeant's course,' he says, 'there were two SAS blokes instructing – Snowy Martin and Kim Scott. Kim was an NCO and was teaching us navigation. I really enjoyed the way he presented and taught; it was very simple and easy to follow. I spoke to him about the regiment and he encouraged me to have a go if I wanted to make a career in the army. That had a significant impact on me.'

However, the chance to apply for the SAS would only come after he had prepared himself with time in the regular army. And there were serious personal and professional impediments to be negotiated before he reached that stage. But at least Palmer was quickly out of the blocks. 'When I re-joined I had to go to Kapooka [NSW] for my boot camp training but because I'd had 10 months of officer training I knew how to march, how to shoot weapons and to navigate,' he says, 'so instead of three months there I did six weeks and was up-squadded to a group that was ready to leave. I marched out of Kapooka and went to the infantry's training centre at Singleton, where I learned to be a good infanteer.'

He enjoyed the experience and quickly made some good mates. 'I found it challenging but not difficult,' he says. 'It sounds like a contradiction, but you're well looked after with accommodation and three square meals a day. You're paid for what you're doing and if you have to move somewhere that's done for you. The challenging part is to push yourself into the unknown, to go to places where you don't know what to expect. You push yourself physically and it's hard work; you walk everywhere with loads on your back and you're experiencing endurance that you haven't had before.

'You've got to learn the language and procedures for different situations. You've got to become tactically aware of things rather than just bumbling along. You have to identify the types of trees, for example, and why they grow there, and why the vegetation is thicker in some places than in others; how to fix anything; how to know where people might be, how to make shelter, protection, fire . . . I was learning stuff that I really felt was interesting and important to me. Some of the basic field craft skills seemed very familiar – almost as though I had known them already. And in fact I had learned a lot of the skills as a kid in the Northern Territory.

'As a boy growing up in the Territory and spending most of my time in the bush, these things came naturally to me – why we see things, how to detect them early and against the backdrop of the bush. My instincts and my friends taught me to identify tracks, follow them and read the signs – which way they move, whether it is fast or slow, and how long ago. The Army taught me shape and size, silhouette and movement, how to "look through" cover and not be fooled by a camouflage effect.

'Working together was also very important. When you have a well-oiled team working together, there is no better feeling. You identify the weak links very quickly and that's what you build up to become the lowest common denominator, and when you complete a task well you know that's pretty cool, it's really satisfying.'

He spent only six weeks in Singleton, where he was up-squadded again to a group that had only four weeks to go. He joined them for a radio test, first aid and the final 9-mile (15-kilometre) run, then was posted as an infantry private to 10 Independent Rifle Company, at Canungra, the army's Jungle Training Centre. Located in the Gold Coast hinterland, Canungra also housed the Land Warfare Centre and 10 IRC provided demonstration troops to its Battle Wing, where sergeants and warrant officers learned combat tactics. As well, they became the 'enemy' in exercises opposing battalion rifle companies who arrived for concentrated training in the field.

'We would be the bad guys,' he says. It was a role he relished, perhaps a little too much for his career prospects.

7

CHALLENGING TIMES

Clint Palmer spent five years at Canungra with 10 IRC. He lived in the single men's quarters on the base and spent much of his free time playing football and golf, and socialising at the Gold Coast. The job – as the 'enemy' – was not particularly demanding provided they followed the script, though it was very tempting at times to ad lib. 'You could a little,' he laughs, 'but not too much, otherwise it would become totally counterproductive and they'd stop the exercise. But many times you'd see the funny side.'

He took promotion courses and was awarded his corporal's stripes. Then he met Vicki, a pretty young strawberry blonde, the sister-in-law of one of his army mates, Jimmy 'Genghis' Khan, who played in Clint's Land Warfare Centre Aussie

Rules team. Vicki was a Tasmanian; she and her family had moved up from Burnie to the Gold Coast in 1975. She often came to the footy and they got together after a game at the base. 'We hit it off and started to go out together,' he says.

By this time he'd completed his three-year tour with 10 IRC and was due to be posted to the 6th Battalion RAR located in Brisbane, then a three-hour drive away. So he contacted the Soldier Career Management Agency (SCMA), and applied for a 'compassionate posting' that would allow him to remain at Canungra. 'It was approved based on the army policy to support members in that position if possible,' he says, 'but it was only for 24 months and I would move after that.'

The new posting had little to recommend it. The Enoggera camp, a grim, featureless dustbowl surrounded by scrub 6 kilometres to the north-west of Brisbane, had been in continuous use by the army since 1908. It boasted sandflies and mosquitoes, ticks, snakes and baking westerly winds. And by 1982 it reflected the rundown state of the army in general.

'There wasn't much happening in those days,' Palmer says. 'It was right in the middle of the so-called drought after Vietnam and before any other commitments came along. It was difficult to maintain any sort of interest and momentum.'

The situation worsened with the 1983 election of the Hawke Labor Government. 'Defence cuts affected us to the point where we had no blank ammunition for our field exercises,' he says. 'I remember deploying to the bush for two weeks with three rounds of ammunition. It was absolutely ridiculous. In our briefings, they said "If you run out of ammunition and the enemy keep advancing on you, shoot them and say, "Bang, Bang". I was going, "Are you kidding? That's schoolkids backyard crap." It was totally embarrassing.

'Honestly, they said, "If you see an armoured vehicle approaching, get the heavy weapon out and go, 'Tank, tank!' and the umpires will know you've engaged the tank." It was probably the worst two weeks of my army career. When we got back we jacked up on them. We told the bosses that this was crap. How the bloody hell do you build a bloody army when you train them with nothing?'

He wanted no part of it. That was when the desire that had lain dormant suddenly returned with renewed urgency: the SAS. There at least he would get the kind of professional support that serious soldiering deserved. He put his hand up for the 1983 selection course that he would have to pass before reaching his goal. And though he was unaware of it at the time, events at Swanbourne had conspired to make it the toughest test yet devised to gain admittance to the unit that prided itself on taking only the best of the best.

By now it had been more than 10 years since the SASR had withdrawn from active service in Vietnam. Initially, they had needed a rest and relished a period of constructive introspection. But they were unprepared for a sudden change of attitude from the military establishment. In a remarkable turnabout, the big army almost overnight had come to resent the 'super-soldiers' of the Special Forces. When the initial post-Vietnam commander, Lieutenant Colonel Ian McFarlane, took over as CO in 1972 this resentment was in full flower. 'SAS was a dirty word in the army,' he says.[15] In the officers' mess the scuttlebutt was that postings to Swanbourne would be sudden death to a military career. Western Command was only interested in finding fault. Army HQ in Canberra had turned its back on the regiment and signalled its attitude unmistakably when it placed the SASR under the newly formed Field Force Command based in Sydney, as far as possible from Swanbourne without actually leaving the Australian continent.

McFarlane responded by playing to the regiment's strengths, ordering long-range exercises in Western Australia. He reinvigorated the training system. He also raised an issue that would prove to be prescient – the need for an Unconventional Warfare Wing designed to respond to urban guerrillas and aggressive kidnappings of Australian citizens both at home and abroad. While waiting for an official response, he organised the transfer to Swanbourne of Captain Tony 'Pancho' Tonna from the Canungra Jungle Training School to develop secret mission teams with skills in demolition, sniping and close-quarter fighting.

About to head off for Operation Anaconda in Afghanistan
– Clint Palmer with Command Sergeant Major Frank Grippe, 2002.

An American helicopter under fire during Operation Anaconda.

Rehearsals continue.
28 Feb. : Payday:
        Continue with Battle
procedure for the "shoot out".
Flew a rehearsal mission today,
wish I had my camera handy,
the views where breath taking.
Up through the snow line and
into the mountains proper —
the biblical world of old
Afghanistan. The mud fortrices
and the people riding donkeys
along narrow mountain trails,
the solitary goat hearders and
the isolated T55 tanks covering
the valleys! This war is not over!
1 Mar.
        Day before combat!

Many briefs and updates —
101 formed up and sung their
unit song- so did 1-87. Roc 6
stood up and said his bit
to stimulate "go get em" syndrom.
The long wait of the night before
has now begun — try to get some
sleep before the helicopter ride
up the valley tomorrow A.M.
2 Mar
        Couldn't sleep much - layd
down for a couple of hours but
kept getting up for coffee.
        Finally made PZ posture
on time and went thru
loading actt etc. We took off
on time and the 1hr 15 flight
was passing slowly.

Palmer's diary entry immediately before Operation Anaconda.

Palmer under fire during Operation Anaconda
– it was a long, long day.

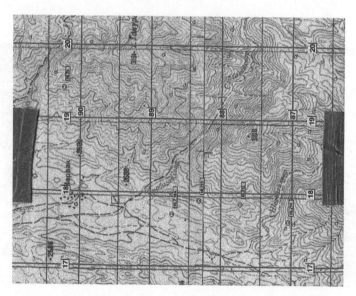

The map Palmer carried during Operation Anaconda – in fact,
copies of Russian maps were used by the Australian and US forces.

Exhausted – Palmer after
Operation Anaconda.

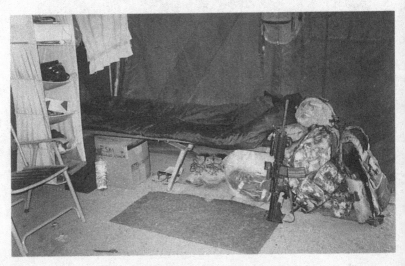

Palmer's quarters in the field.

CLINT –

GLAD YOU + YOUR GUYS COVERED
OUR BACKS IN THE LZ ON 2 MAR.

THANKS,
CAPTAIN ED LENGEL
66TH RESCUE SQUADRON
GECKO 11 FLIGHT LEAD

Some Americans appreciated the Australians' efforts during
Operation Anaconda!

The day after a contact in Afghanistan.

At Bagram Airbase, Afghanistan.

A mediation session with some locals and our forces.

At the firing range – Tarin Kot, southern Afghanistan.

The day after a contact in Afghanistan.

Breakfast with then Minister for Foreign Affairs Kevin Rudd
in Afghanistan, 3 March 2011.

In Baghdad, Iraq, December 2008.

However, his successor in December 1973, Lieutenant Colonel Neville Smethurst, had a much more conventional approach. He reoriented the unit to conduct operations behind enemy lines in the event of an invasion or when operating overseas. He renamed it the Guerrilla Warfare Wing. He eliminated its clandestine flavour and opened it up to all SAS personnel to undertake its courses. In time, McFarlane's initiative would be revived as a counter-terrorism asset, but for the moment the regiment found itself languishing while it cast about in a hostile environment for a new raison d'être.

Smethurst turned his attention within and tackled the problem of attracting good-quality officers who could retain the respect of the highly trained troopers under their command. In 1974, he inaugurated the first Officers Selection Course which was just as physically gruelling as that faced by privates and NCOs, and even more intellectually demanding. According to regiment historian David Horner, once the new system was in place, 'There could no longer be any doubts among the soldiers about the quality of their officers. The introduction of the course was to have a profound effect on the quality of future officers in the SAS.'

The CO then dealt with the clique of senior NCOs who had come to believe – with some justice – that they 'ran the show'. Some had been with the regiment since its inception and were not only set in their ways but were blocking the promotion of younger and less hidebound replacements. He developed a system that allowed warrant officers and senior NCOs to be posted out of the regiment as infantry CSMs without losing their SAS status, and with the capacity to return to more senior and influential positions in the regiment.

But while the notorious Australian tall poppy syndrome was at work among David Stirling's 'fossilised shits' within the military bureaucracy, the SASR's international reputation was providing a balm to the regimental ego. Special Forces units from Britain (Special Boat Squadron and Royal Marine Commandos), the United States (Navy SEALs), New Zealand (SAS), Malaysia (Special Services Regiment) and Indonesia all initiated visits to Campbell Barracks, and issued invitations to the Australians for reciprocal collaboration and joint exercises. They discovered in this way that the British 22 SAS Regiment was already developing a counter-terrorism capability along the lines Ian McFarlane had proposed.

Smethurst also introduced the SAS to Africa through an arrangement with the Red Cross to pay the salary of one of his troopers, who would be attached to their humanitarian operation in drought-ravaged Ethiopia. He would provide 'eyes-on' intelligence to the regiment that would be useful in the event of an emergency action in the Dark Continent, though it would be a long time before this initiative bore fruit.

At the start of 1976, Mike Jeffrey, the young officer who had escaped the jaws of a crocodile in Montague Sound when it climbed aboard his rubber dinghy 16 years previously, returned as the regiment's commanding officer. He had served in the SASR several times during his rise through the ranks, most recently as adjutant in 1966. Since then he had attended the British Army Staff College and been the CO of the Pacific Islands Regiment in Papua New Guinea.

Now a lieutenant colonel, his initial months as CO of the regiment were tarnished by two fatal training casualties: first a parachuting mishap; then a trooper's fall down a coal storage pit during a night raid. Indeed, the regiment would continue to lose many more men through tough training operations than in enemy combat. However, Jeffrey's commitment to the highest standards was unremitting, and in 1977 long-range patrols covered more than 65,000 square kilometres of Australia's north and west in a single exercise involving 200 SAS officers and men. His command was judged a success and helped bring the regiment back into favour within the military establishment.

This process accelerated in 1978 when urban terrorists of the Ananda Marga sect attacked the Commonwealth Heads of Government Meeting at Sydney's Hilton Hotel. By now Jeffrey had become the driving force in the Joint and Special Warfare unit in Canberra, and he proposed the formation of a counter-terrorism Tactical Assault Group (TAG) within the SASR. The recommendation was accepted and Jeffrey was promoted to become the first director of Special Action Forces in Canberra.

Lieutenant Colonel Reg Beesley, who had commanded an SAS squadron in Vietnam, had been appointed CO of the regiment in October 1977 and it fell to him to develop a training system to produce a counter-terrorism team within the unit. Its role was expanded in August 1979 in a directive from the chief of general staff providing an establishment of three officers and 26 soldiers. Their tasks included an aggressive response to terrorist groups involved in hijacking aircraft, kidnapping, assassination and the invasion of public buildings. They would operate under the codeword 'Gauntlet'.

Training began in March 1980 at special facilities erected at Campbell Barracks. These included a building known as the 'killing house' where trainees used live ammunition in submachine-guns fitted with torches. In the darkened rooms they would fire at 'terrorists' caught in the torchlight before returning to a waiting room with their colleagues. The force was fully operational two months later.

In December 1979, Soviet Union troops had entered Afghanistan at the Kabul government's request to quell a widespread rebellion. They quickly took control of the major urban centres, military bases and strategic installations. However, the presence of Soviet troops enraged the Afghan nationalists, and the rebellion spread and deepened. Babrak Karmal, Afghanistan's new president, charged the Soviets with causing an increase in the unrest, and demanded that its 40th Army step in and quell the rebellion, as his own army had proved untrustworthy. Thus, Soviet troops found themselves drawn into fighting against urban uprisings, tribal armies and sometimes against mutinous Afghan Army units.

The Americans took advantage of the situation by arming the Mujahideen rebels against their Cold War foes, thus beginning a process that would eventually draw the United States into a disastrous semi-religious conflict, seemingly with no resolution in sight more than 30 years later. The Australian Government and military leadership received intelligence briefings from the Americans and these were shared at an operational level with the SAS command.

By then Beesley had been succeeded by Lieutenant Colonel Rod Curtis, who realised the demands being made on the regiment required their raising a third Sabre squadron.

But, once again, the 'fossilised shits' of middle management raised their ugly heads and denied him the funding to raise the new squadron quickly and efficiently. Indeed, it would not be fully operational until the end of 1982.

Curtis was also concerned about the lack of a firm direction for the regiment's operations. 'There remains no clear perception as to how SASR should be employed operationally in time of war,' he wrote. 'SASR is now covering the broad span of Special Action Forces skills and techniques. This has resulted in veneer specialisation and degradation of primary war skills.'[16] He proposed an 'authoritative document' setting out the unit's tasks and operational control in time of war. The tasks would be 'outside the scope of conventional forces', but he suggested that tactical operations, like those undertaken in South Vietnam, might also be required.

When he submitted his paper to army HQ it drew a quick response from the CO of the 1st Commando Regiment based in Sydney, Lieutenant Colonel Peter McDougall. A long-serving SAS officer, McDougall called for an appreciation of the operational standing of the two Special Forces units, thereby setting in train a debate that has only recently been resolved.

Curtis was succeeded by Lieutenant Chris Roberts in December 1982. He had fought with the SASR in Vietnam, and in the late 1970s had commanded 1 Squadron before taking a position under Colonel Jeffrey in the Directorate of Special Action Forces. He responded to McDougall's concerns by sending members of the Tactical Assault Group to Sydney to run special courses for the Commando Regiment. He also set up a training cell in 1 Squadron to conduct four counter-terrorism (CT) courses each year. He oversaw major exercises in Australia and Papua New Guinea, some independent, others in concert with army and air force units.

By the time he relinquished command in 1985, the regiment had not only regained its *esprit de corps* and the grudging respect of the big army, but it had also brought its entrance selection trial to a new and exhausting level, where at least 70 per cent of applicants would almost certainly fall by the wayside. Among them, in 1983, would be Corporal Clint Palmer.

8

PARACHUTES

is preparation for the course left much to be desired. He was unaware how far his standards had slipped from those of the eager and ambitious career soldier who had joined up seven years ago. 'I did a little bit of running and fitness work, but not as much as I probably could have,' he says. 'I relied on my natural ability to maintain fitness through football and stuff to get through.'

He was also unprepared for the conditions that prevailed during winter at Singleton, where the course was now conducted. Almost as soon as it began he developed a chest infection, and although he struggled on he was pulled out of the course on medical grounds. In fact, this was fortunate. If he'd simply given up, he would not have been permitted to try again. This allowed him a second chance, and there was no way he would allow himself to fail next time.

He was lucky too that a group of his mates from 6 RAR also decided to make a bid for the SASR and they were able to train together.

'The first couple of months after I got back I had a little break and then I started training in earnest,' he says. 'I did 10 months of intensive training. There were six of us from the unit who trained together. I was in 4th Platoon, B company, and all the other guys were from Recon Platoon in Support company.'

They were good mates. They played football and water polo together. And they trained like men possessed. They worked out in the gym. They went to aerobics classes four nights a week. They did route marches carrying extra heavy packs. They ran in all their webbing carrying their rifles at the ready. 'I would run five nights a week,' he says. 'I'd get home from the aerobics class and I'd go for an 8 k run carrying a 20-pound iron bar.'

By now he had moved out of army digs and flatted with his sister Nita and her husband Stu Amos in suburban Indooroopilly, not far from the orphanage to which his father and his uncles had been consigned during the war years. His runs took him through Brisbane's leafy southern suburbs, out to the Queensland University and back.

'By the end of it,' he says, 'I was that fit I was jumping out of my skin.'

The regiment had abandoned the two-year experiment with an eastern states testing ground and when selection time arrived they flew the six Enoggera candidates in a C-130 to the Pearce RAAF Base north of Perth then loaded them onto the back of a truck for the long drive to the Northam Army Camp, Clint's military alma mater.

It was a warm March, and the Queensland contingent was eager to get to grips with the ordeal. 'It was a full three weeks,' he says, 'and the course – like the weather – was completely different. It was the end of our summer, so still quite warm, not cold and wet and the middle of bloody winter like the previous year. Northam had some hills but not quite as bad as around Singleton, so the environment was far more conducive to positive results.'

However, there was a catch. The CO, Chris Roberts, had decided that as part of his program to expand and improve the selection process they would make a television documentary of the course. So not only did they design it to be tougher than all previous years, but they often required the exhausted candidates to repeat elements of the trial for the cameras.

'I'll never forget it,' he says. 'They were torturing us. Instead of doing an hour to an hour and a half of PT, it was two hours. They wanted to really portray the toughness of it. We had these guys running around saying, "Can we just do that again, please? Run up the hill and jump over the log, crawl back under the pipe then jump over the pipe again so we can get the shot right. Now let's try a different angle so we can get the sun coming up . . ." They called it *Battle for the Golden Road*.'

After three weeks, the ranks of the candidates had thinned. Some had dropped by the wayside through sheer exhaustion; others had cracked mentally and refused to continue; still others had been removed by the directing staff (DS) running the course. Not so the Queensland contingent. 'All six of us passed,' Palmer says. 'In fact, we were all in the top 10. It was awesome.'

'It was a mixed feeling,' he says, 'Relief and immense satisfaction, but disbelief that you'd done it. It was like everything else that you'd done beforehand didn't matter anymore. Because now you were at the bottom of the ladder of a brand new chance in life and everything was starting fresh. But the start point was up there well above where you'd been anyway. So you're going, "Yes, there is a God."'

'I suddenly understood why it was so important that I'd made the decision not to stay where I was, because I knew now where the real challenge of soldiering was. It's at this level. I take nothing away from the infantry battalions and the conventional army guys, because they do a hell of a job and they're all good people. But from an individual perspective, to have goals and to make the grade, so to speak, to step off on to a platform which is now quite elevated meant there was now a standard to live up to. There was pressure, an expectation to learn and to endure and develop in the pursuit of excellence. Everything you did now had to be done well; not just good, not just to get through; but to be done well.'

Although passing selection opened the gates to Campbell Barracks and the elite of Australia's Special Forces, it was no guarantee of permanent membership. That would come only after the successful completion of a series of 'reinforcement' courses initiating the newcomers into the special skills and techniques of the SAS. That was when he realised just how different the regiment was from the big army that spawned it. 'The mentality is extremely different,' he says. 'The maturity level is different, and that's simply because the role and the tasks are different and much more demanding. Everything you do is modelled around real-time capability. You can't half train for something which is so important it has to be done to the best possible level.' And after he threw himself wholeheartedly into his work he found ready acceptance. He successfully completed the cycle in August 1984.

Almost 30 years later, after all the highs and lows, the emotional bond to the regiment remains as powerful as ever. 'It's a brethren,' he says. 'It's a group that once you belong, it's very dear to you. You depend on everybody around you. The trust has got to be there. When the axe falls, it falls swiftly and ruthlessly. The Mafia's the same. The parallels are there. But of course we're on the overt side of the law. We're out there, the legitimate force and the force of choice by government. We are representative of the nation. We're part of the army but we operate independently and it has to be that way because you've canvassed the forces to extract the best of what is available to suit the purposes of the regiment. You need fuel for the fire and you've got to get high-grade fuel for the fire to burn bright. And this is the regiment, a bunch of really talented ordinary people who work hard to achieve extraordinary results.'

All recruits immediately lose the rank they achieved outside – another sharp indicator that they had transitioned to a new military paradigm. Trooper Palmer's first posting was to 3 Squadron. He would remain in that active Sabre squadron for almost three years. Much of the work was hard training – roping, shooting, driving and patrolling – but some time was spent jungle training in the North Queensland rainforest. 'We then moved to New Guinea and did an exercise there,' he says. 'As part of our acclimatisation and hearts and minds work, we split the squadron up into groups and all went off to different areas to do projects. My group climbed Mount Victoria.'

Originally known as the Great Mountain, it rises 4,038 metres (13,248 feet), to the highest point in the Owen Stanley Ranges. There had been several attempts to scale it by British colonialists in the 1880s. All failed after clashes with local villagers until the British administrator, Sir William McGregor, led an elaborate expedition in 1889, and on reaching the peak named it for his sovereign.

'We left Port Moresby and we flew by helicopter into a little village called Manumu in the upper Stanleys, about two days walk from Kokoda,' Clint says. 'It took us six days to get up and two days to get down. It was pretty testing experience. We left one fellow at about the 11,000 feet mark. He came down with altitude sickness so we rugged him up and left him there with the two Papua New Guinea Defence Force guides. The rest of us went up to the top, and when we came back he was okay.

'It was a pretty tough climb because the air was so thin. We had to traverse up a creek line for two days to get to the turnoff, find an overgrown track and follow it. Approaching the summit there was a very slippery, wet grass, mossy-type area. We were on hands and knees crawling up to this little plateau that thinned down to a razorback ridge about 2 feet wide and about 20 to 25 metres long. On one side, it was about 400 or 500 feet straight down and on the other side, it was about 3,000 feet straight down – pretty terrifying.

'When we got to the top there's a rock cairn and a little tin with notes in it. We discovered that that we were only the seventh group ever to be up there. We had taken our weapons and full packs up, but left them at base camp at 11,500 feet. On the way back down, the weather started closing in. The clouds started to build up, and going back across this ridge it was clear and then quite suddenly, whiteout. Instantaneously we all had vertigo, loss of balance and disorientation, so I dropped and stayed down on my hands and knees for about 30 seconds and pop, it was clear as a bell again.

'It was basically a shake-down exercise, getting to know each other, going through certain procedures and just spending time together for a week or so. We got an aerial resupply at about day four. It was quite cold and we tried to light fires, but the air was so wet and damp and there were no trees, no dead wood at that altitude.'

The climb was a highlight of his early years. But the element he was really looking forward to was parachute training. Those childhood experiences at Batchelor airfield had made an indelible impression.

Leonardo da Vinci is generally credited as being 'the father of the parachute' with his famous drawing in 1485 of a device designed to allow people to escape from tall buildings on fire. However, his design was not replicated for more than five centuries, when an Englishman, Adrian Nicholas, put it to the test (successfully) in July 2000. The French – who supplied the name – were the principal pioneers in the 18th and 19th centuries, usually from hot air balloons. It was another Englishman, Robert Cocking, who had the dubious distinction of becoming the first fatality when he leapt from a balloon at 5,000 feet with his homemade device in 1837.

The First World War provided a quantum leap in parachute development, with the German Air Force equipping planes with static-line-operated parachutes. Pilots wearing only a harness simply leapt out and after falling a few feet a line fastened outside the cockpit would deploy the parachute. There were many complications: spinning aircraft would snag a deploying parachute; tumbling wreckage sometimes tore apart canopy fabric or suspension lines; and flames racing along a fuselage would damage the canopy. But many World War I aviators and balloonists did ultimately owe their lives to parachutes.

In 1918, the US Army formed a Parachute Section at Wilbur Wright Field in Dayton, Ohio, and soon developed a practical parachute for emergency escape from aircraft. Parachutes from around the world were drop-tested and the static-line-deployed parachutes were replaced with manually operated free-fall rigs that could be operated by a user after falling clear of a crippled machine

The development of modern parachutes deployed at high speeds and high altitudes started in the 1930s, and the Germans used mass airborne troops to support the invasion of Holland, Belgium and Luxembourg. They dropped 35,000 airborne troops on the isle of Crete in 1942 and on D-Day some 24,000 Allied paratroopers were deployed. Since then there had been a continuous development of equipment and techniques.

Unfortunately Palmer would have to wait another 18 months before he was able to make his first free-fall jump with the regiment. It was particularly annoying because he had already done some civilian jumps and loved it. But he couldn't jump with his troop until he'd gained the advanced free-fall qualification, and when exercises involved parachuting he had to take the vehicle out to meet them on the ground. 'I was totally frustrated,' he says, 'because the parachute school only had a certain capacity for students and there was a backlog. It was a year and a half before I got on my Military Free-fall (MFF) course.'

His first civilian jump had been with his brothers during a Christmas holiday back in WA from Canungra. The drop zone was at Dale River, a two-hour drive along the Brookton Highway south of Perth. 'My brothers had started jumping the year before so I thought I'd jump on the bandwagon, so to speak,' he says. 'I thought if they can do it, it can't be that hard.' That morning he'd completed two or three hours of theory on how a parachute opened, how to land and what to do if trouble struck. It was very basic and was accompanied by plenty of friendly banter from brothers Blake and Dean. As they took off, Clint was closest to the door. It took five or six minutes to get to jumping height at 2,500 feet. 'It wasn't that long at all,' he laughs. 'It was an eternity. There was lots of anticipation, lots of adrenaline, lots of nervous, anxious moments until it all happens.

'When we reached the jump point the jump master reached around, opened the door, and gave me the command to go,' Palmer says. 'I went.'

It was a static-line deployment and the 'chute would take between three and five seconds to open as the wind inflated it under pressure. An old round model, it was on his back with the emergency on his belly connected by a harness system. 'I remember it very clearly,' he says. 'The high point of the exit was actually hanging on the strut without being blown off and looking back at the instructor waving and giving the chop. I'd had some second thoughts about it on the way up but now I thought, "Too late, I'm here; I've got to go."'

He'd been instructed to count the seconds as the parachute followed the laws of physics with the air forcing its way into the canopy and inflating it. He followed the drill – one thousand, two thousand, three thousand . . . then the pressure suddenly increased on his harness. 'They were pretty anxious seconds,' he says. 'The wind hits your chest and pushes you away from the plane. Then I looked up and realised exactly how it's supposed to be. The nice, cold breeze on the face was lovely because it was quite warm on the ground that day. It's quiet and it's peaceful and you can see everything for miles. You try and take it all in and it's, "Wow, this is fun." I think I gave a bit of a "Yahoo!"

'They put me out at a place upwind of the target, so the idea was to turn, face the target area, fly down at an appropriate height, turn the parachute back into the wind so you nullify the airspeed of the parachute, and come down soft as you can. On my side of the Brookton Highway, there was a state forest and on the other were wheat fields and the airfield. There was a little shed, the runway, windsock and the white X on the ground. I'm going, "Yeah, yeah, it's all good. I've seen all that." It's a different perspective, I think it's called the isometric view, but when you're on top, looking down, it's quite different.

'I was hoping I wasn't going to go into the forest, but the winds were all blowing in that direction. The barbed wire fences around the wheat fields were a bit of a worry, because if you landed on a fence you were in trouble. I actually saw that happen once and a girl broke her leg. However, I made it down okay, maybe 100 metres off the X but on the right side of the highway.

'It was a relatively soft landing because you bend your legs enough for them to act as a shock absorber. It's just a matter of setting up in the right position and allowing your body to collapse and roll at the same time, and if you do that you don't get hurt. I had this grin like the Cheshire Cat on my face for hours afterwards. The first jump is one of those things that scares the hell out of you. You'll either never do it again, or it's instantly addictive. It's a bite that grabs you and says, "Yeah, come on, let's go do that again." And that was the case with me. I knew it . . . immediately.'

However, by this time Palmer had decided to try for selection and he knew that if successful he'd get the best military training. 'I knew I'd have ample time to go parachuting after that,' he says. 'But what I did do was buy a parachute in anticipation. My brother sold me his and he bought a new one. I didn't realise I'd have to wait for nearly two years – 1985 – before I made my first jump in the regiment.' Nor did he have the slightest inkling that in a career of more than 1,500 jumps he would face death several times and eventually become the regiment's most expert parachute instructor at the national parachute school. But in the basic reinforcement parachuting course after selection he was already aware of a powerful attraction.

He was immediately struck by the difference in the military's approach to the task. 'The civil drop zone is all about money and turnover – getting people through the doors; whereas the military system is concentrated on the safety and actual capability,' he says. 'Parachuting to the ground is simply a means to an end. It's to get guys to a place where they're able to do their job. So the safety aspects in training become paramount. For two weeks we were in this stinking hot hangar in Williamtown doing some 50 plus lessons of 40 minutes each.

'You have to learn every single lesson. But going back, being the student for two weeks' was like, "Oh my God, why can't we just go jump?" Having jumped before, all you want is to do it again and not go through all the procedural lessons and stuff,' he says. 'But there were guys there who obviously had no idea what was going on; it was all new to them. So the level of training is aimed at the lowest common denominator and the thoroughness and the repetition and the consolidation of each phase of training is important. It becomes instinctive; it's like weapon handling – your skills have to be polished to the point where you do things without even thinking about it. Parachuting is no different because if you stuff it up that has fatal consequences.'

Finally, he was up in an aircraft – a C-130 – and ready to leap into the blue. And it was just as thrilling as he'd remembered it. 'The first two or three descents were what they call "Clean fatigue", so you carried no weapons or other equipment,' he says. 'That was so you understood how the parachute flies, the sensation of it opening, getting used to where everything is. You practise steering your parachute and your landing technique. Landing is vital and you practise coming in from all points of the compass. You set yourself up for all the landing contingencies.'

He moved easily from the static-line deployment to free-fall, where parachutists jump in teams and manoeuvre for a period before opening their chutes. 'My first one was from a C-130,' he says. 'The jump was from 1,000 feet. The earlier jump, from 2,500 feet, was from a small Cessna that struggled to fit five people on board . . . this was luxury. But it's more than you need for the parachute to open and for you to land safely. The lower you are to the ground, the less interference the wind is going to have to blow you off the intended target area. Lower is more accurate but this means that the aircraft has to be lined up in exactly the right place in order to let you out.

'There's a continuous dispatch of jumpers; they just go one behind the other so you'll have your "exit" close together and they'll land close together. The time-delayed dispatch, which is normally two seconds, gives you a spread of 120 feet between people,' he says. 'The military paratroop aircraft are designed to put people out of each side, simultaneously. So there is a chance of people going at the same time and coming back and colliding. It does happen from time to time, but you're taught collision drills so that if that does occur, then you take the appropriate action to minimise the effect of the entanglement. That's why the ground training in military parachuting is two weeks long.

'On this occasion I think I was second out. I was too busy concentrating on my own actions, so I can't be sure, but the guys who hadn't jumped before were shouting, "Yahoo!" and "Yee-haw!" This was regarded as unprofessional and they were told in no uncertain terms, "Okay, guys, you don't have to do that." Simple reason – down the track, we do tactical jumps – you don't go screaming to let the enemy know you're coming.

'You have guys who go out in the wrong position and their body starts to twist. Then the parachute comes out when they're twisted. It will still open but you've got to do what they call a "bicycle kick" and force the risers apart, which winds you back out. That's the emergency drills you do in the military – twists and entanglements. If you get a twist you look up, see what the twist is, force the risers, and kick until you're out and the canopy is okay.

'It often happened to me. Some twists are more severe than others. I've seen twists all the way up the lines on rare occasions, but more often it's very temporary; as the air goes into the canopy it's forcing it open and forcing the twist to undo. It's quite dizzying as it comes out. Most times, particularly when you go out the side door, you're going to experience some sort of twist. It might be half a twist or maybe one full twist, but if you reach up and push as hard as you can and kick at the same time, it'll come apart. Sometimes there's no time to set up for landing, but there's a fair chance that you'll go out and the parachute will come out deployed with no twists. That's a great jump.'

'We were quite a good course,' he says. 'We went through the drills, did our seven jumps, the first and second clean fatigue, the third and fourth jumps with combat equipment. These were all-day jumps. The fifth jump was combat equipment, continuous full sides, so instead of being a counted exit, it's the whole side of the aircraft – all 20 guys out at once. Then the sixth jump was not from the side door but over the back of the ramp. That was luxury, and we used an MC1 parachute, which was a steerable one. The ones before were non-steerable round things that went where the wind took you.

Then came the last jump, at night, and that was something else. 'It was probably scary for some people who have problems with the night or the dark anyway, let alone compounding that with all the things you need to do on a parachute jump. I've seen some people having difficulty with that. But for the normal guy and professional, well-trained digger it wasn't a problem. You'd be surprised how much you can see in the air at night. Your vision becomes much clearer for some reason. I reckon it's the adrenaline, the blood starts racing and the rods and cones are doing things in your eyeballs.

'You become very aware of what's going on because your body naturally compensates for the darkness and tries its best to see and help you out, so to speak. But of course on pitch-black nights the biggest struggle is landing, getting that depth perception, knowing when to set up for it. So the drill in night jumps is turn, face the wind, set up for landing then wait until you've arrived. The biggest, single, scariest point is hitting the ground before you're ready for it.'

The other great difference from civilian parachuting was the load the soldiers carried as they left the aircraft – an M-16 weapon, chest webbing and a back pack. 'The pack and webbing are normally packed together in a bag, which is attached to you between your legs,' he says, 'and your weapon is slung to the side. Originally, the teaching was to drop the pack separately. You put everything into the pack and just jumped with your weapon on you and a spare magazine in your pocket. Later you'd take water, food, ammo and some navigation aids on your person. So if you did get into trouble on the ground, at least you had something to eat, something to drink, a map, a GPS, some ammo to get you out of immediate trouble. The new system with the weapon attached to the back pack is preferable. But obviously this is all going to be dictated by the security of the drop zone that you jump into. If it's a secure area, there's no reason why you couldn't put all your personal effects into your main pack and jump.'

9

COMMIT TO THE SKY GODS

Clint Palmer's PNG mountain-climbing exercise was part of a pivotal change in direction for the regiment. Most of its older members who had fought in Vietnam had moved on; its leadership had developed a strong counter-terrorist capability; it was now looking beyond Australia's borders once again and giving a high priority to developing its war role.

Paradoxically, the new CO appointed in July 1985 was himself a holdover from Vietnam, where he had been 2IC of a squadron in 1970. However, Lieutenant Colonel Terry Nolan at 40 had spent the intervening years carving a career path through the Special Action Forces directorate. He was not only uniquely qualified for the job, he also broke the mould by being the first graduate of the Portsea Officer Cadet

School (as opposed to the high-status RMC Duntroon) to command the SASR.

He was fortunate in having a Minister for Defence in Kim Beazley who defied the Labor stereotype with his unabashed enthusiasm for the task. And as a Western Australian, the minister was more than happy to throw his considerable weight behind the SAS cause. In April 1986, he announced a $22 million upgrade in facilities at Swanbourne, the Bindoon training area and at Gin Gin airfield. These included a new close-quarter battle range complex at Campbell Barracks and special counter-terrorist sniper facilities at Bindoon.

However, despite this active – even generous – support, the regiment suffered from the most debilitating circumstance in the soldier's dictum: an extended period of uninterrupted peace. With no war to fight, the CO substituted a range of increasingly demanding challenges to fill the gap. Mountain climbing was the forerunner of a series of climbs involving the regiment and incorporating New Zealand's Mount Cook, America's Mount McKinley and Kenya's Mount Kilimanjaro, and culminating in a successful assault on the big one, Mount Everest, in 7 May 1988. Major Pat Cullinan, who had pioneered the climbing expeditions in the regiment, reached the summit with a civilian, Pat Byrnes, although by then he had transferred to 1st Commando Regiment.

Terry Nolan had been succeeded by Lieutenant Colonel Jim Wallace earlier that year. Wallace had previously served as both a troop and squadron commander in the regiment and would make a strong showing as CO. His later Christian views and activities as head of the Australian Christian Lobby were not then on show. He was highly regarded, not least by Clint Palmer. 'He didn't parade any of that,' Palmer says. 'He was the complete professional. He made a point of spending time where he could with the men. I recall when we were in Darwin after a CT exercise and we all went to the Vic Hotel for a beer. Jim came in and bought the whole squadron a drink, talked to the boys and left us to enjoy ourselves. Jim would follow up on things too. I asked him a question about a new weapon system once and he said, "I don't know the answer, Clint, but I'll get back to you when I do." Three months later, he approached me and gave me an answer – that impressed me. He was a guy who really invigorated a lot of things and initiated the remuneration tribunal to come and reassess the pay.'

This followed the adoption of CO Neville Smethurst's plan that NCOs be rotated to the big army for a period before returning to the SASR. 'Blokes didn't want to leave Swanbourne to go back to the other army, do various jobs and come back a couple of years later because they were going to lose money,' Clint says. 'At the time we were paid a little bit more. It was enough for guys to want to stay because they were marrying, having kids, buying houses, and committing themselves financially. If they went over east, they lost money and wouldn't be able to keep up payments on the house.

'On the other hand they're working hard for long hours and spending a lot of time away from home so maybe they should be entitled to a bit more money. So we put together this package, Jim Wallace went to Canberra, lobbied Defence and the government to put this remuneration thing together. We did a whole bunch of demonstrations on every aspect of where the unit was and its capability and we convinced them to give us a pay rise.'

Wallace also understood the importance of development from within, and expanded on Terry Nolan's mountaineering expeditions to extend capability and maintain morale. He encouraged troopers, NCOs and officers to propose projects that would benefit themselves and the unit. Clint says, 'Two fellows came up with a plan to travel through the countries that we don't normally go to in Asia – Laos, Cambodia, Burma – by low-level means: canoe, boat, train, bus. It was anything but the tourist thing. It was an actual integration into society as they travelled and worked their way around. For example, they'd go the length of the Mekong River in a dugout, all that sort of stuff. It was approved and they were given the funds to do it, and off they went for three or four months.'

It's a practice that has continued in various forms. 'We were getting our guys into regions where not many people had been, let alone someone from Defence,' he says. 'They bring back fresh information of how it actually is out there.'

Like the rest of the regiment, Clint had been affected by the routines of peacetime soldiering. While he retained all his early enthusiasm for the task, there was no real outlet for the combat and particularly the counter-terrorism skills he had acquired. 'We had to maintain a [CT] squadron capability to deploy at short notice,' he says. 'We were on four hours' notice to move into action.' But months and years would pass without any call to arms. 'There were satellite skirmishes, but nothing the Australian Government was involved in during the late 80s.'

However, he relished the discipline that had so attracted the founder of the SAS, David Stirling, all those years ago in North Africa: parachuting. The frustrations of those initial years when he'd had to wait endlessly, it seemed, to attend the parachute school had been swept away in October 1985 when at last his number came up. His was the final military free-fall course to be conducted at Williamtown before the move to Nowra.

'It was important to knuckle down and do the best I could, despite having some experience already,' he says. 'It had been 18 months since I last had the taste of military parachuting, and that was low-level static jumping. I was so looking forward to doing my MFF course so I could free-fall into exercises and train with the rest of the troop. I couldn't get to Williamtown quick enough, and 25 October 1985 was day one of the course.

'We had some fairly serious training to do before the staff would consider us competent enough to throw us out on our own.'

The world of high-altitude parachuting is a far cry from climbing into the back of an aircraft, levelling out at 1,000 feet and falling out the back. As terrifying as it may be, exiting at 10,000 feet and falling for 40 seconds, then deploying the parachute manually at 3,000 feet can become addictive. The next couple of days saw repetitive training, learning about the parachute, the instruments and other kit needed to conduct MFF. Terms like "relative air", "burble" "track", "wave off", "stability" and "activate" were all part of a new language they were all soaking up. Hanging in the flight trainers, smashing the emergency procedures and going through all the drills, until it was second nature crammed their days. 'I recall not sleeping much on the night of 27 October,' he says. 'I lay there going through the drills again and again in my head.

'The parachute system they used then was known as "fore and aft" because the main parachute was worn on the back, and the reserve was on the chest. Called an MC-2, it was simply a normal static-line MC-1 configured for free-fall. The reserve was a 26-foot "super steerable" with a pair of Smiths altimeters mounted on the top flap. We had two alts, because at that time one couldn't rely on one alone, such was the lack of faith in the accuracy of them. They were fairly chunky things about the size of a grapefruit and heavy as hell.'

The emergency reserve deployment drill included turning the head off to one side to avoid the alts flying up and hitting the face with the parachute – although some were caught out from time to time.

The first four descents were on the MC-2. Then they graduated to the sports car of the sky, the MC-3 or Para Commander as it was known in the civilian sport. This was a fast manoeuvrable canopy which had drive slots and stabilisers and could turn a 360-degree circle in 5 to 8 seconds. 'Wow – couldn't wait for that one,' he says. 'My instructor was a guy called Laurie "Truck" Sams, an accomplished skydiver and respected in the international parachuting community.' Sams was one of only two or three Australians who jumped into the Olympic Stadium in Seoul at the opening of the 1988 Olympics, and had been inducted into the renowned "Golden Knights", the US Army Parachute Display Team. He had an SAS background and had served in Vietnam with the unit. 'He and I struck up a strong friendship which has endured to this day', Palmer says.

'The sun came up as usual on 28 October, but to me this was no ordinary day – I was about to commit my flesh to the sky gods! I was nervous but excited; my mind raced at 100 miles an hour; all I wanted to do was get that first one out of the way. Truck pulled me aside and gave me the descent briefing, and we went over it again just to confirm we were on the same page. It was all very simple; he would back off the ramp, holding onto me; at the same time I would dive so we left the aircraft as one. We would hold the exit, flatten out and I would do two dummy pulls of the ripcord, concurrently maintaining height awareness with alt checks; and I would deploy the main parachute at 4,000 feet, at which time he would let go of me and fall away to 3,000 feet and open.'

Everything went well leading up to the exit. Then: "Ready, set, go!" and he let go of me as we went out! I didn't have time to be terrified,' Palmer says. 'I had too many things to think about. My mind was racing; on the one hand I was staying with the game plan; on the other also thinking, "You prick, you were never going to hang onto me at all!" He sat there in the sky only two feet away from me smiling and giving me the thumbs up until I opened. From then on I understood that if you commit to leaving a perfectly good aircraft, then you and you only are responsible for your own actions'.

That first jump catapulted him into a new dimension, and made him acutely aware of the importance of detail and accuracy of information. The rest of the jump went without incident, and when he gathered up the parachute and walked back to the bus, Truck stood there with a big grin on his face and said, 'Well, how did that go?' and they both burst into laughter.

The next couple of jumps went well. They then did 12 more jumps on the MC-3 before the test of leaping out with combat equipment [CE] comprising pack, rifle and webbing attached. By now, however, most did very well and the skill level was quite high for so few descents.

'We went on to make nine more CE jumps before the last descent and qualified on 15 November', he says. 'In among all the fun of the fair, we lost a few days due to bad weather, which meant we didn't reach our target number of around 50 jumps. But we all went home with 31 jumps and a qualification, and more importantly, I could now fit in with the rest of the troop and be included in any activity that would present in the future.'

In 1988 the army purchased a number of new parachutes for trial, and they were sent across to Perth for us to use and report back on. The Parachute Training School had done extensive trials already, and wanted the opinion of the user unit. They deployed to Learmonth for a couple of weeks and gave them a thorough workout. While waiting for the arrival of the new lot of parachutes, Palmer's patrol was tasked with a parachute insertion patrol in North Queensland. The jump was planned to use the trial parachutes, but that didn't happen, so they had to put up with being the last ever group in the army to use the old round MC-3 parachute for a tactical patrol insertion.

'We did a rehearsal jump at RAAF Pearce on 5 October 1988, at night with full CE,' he says. 'This night would be one of the most memorable jumps of my career. The exit went fine; free-fall was fine and then the opening – not fine! The pilot chute flopped over the nose of the canopy and out through the right-hand stabiliser, causing the canopy to dive to the right and commence to wind up.

'Immediately I went into survival mode; by the third rotation the blood had started to pool in my feet and they felt like anchors dragging behind me. Then it happened, the drill kicked in: "Legs back, covers, cut, covers, pull." I chopped the main and deployed the reserve, which opened beautifully and brought me down safe and well. I was cursing the fact we didn't have the new rigs, because in my mind that would never have happened if we were on the square trial parachutes.'

On 8 October his patrol was inserted into a drop zone somewhere in Queensland, and all five landed in trees, writing off all the main canopies. This was a fitting end to a parachute which was the forerunner to the square parachutes of the modern era.

•

That was just the beginning. Palmer revelled in the discipline. 'We would conduct parachute continuation training exercises for up to six weeks, at times rotating all qualified members of the regiment through a regime of jumps which would normally take a week or so to complete,' he says. 'We would travel to places in the Western Australian countryside from Katanning in the south, Kalgoorlie in the East and Learmonth in the north. Parachuting consisted of static-line land descents, military free-fall jumps and intentional water descents.

'Water descents were normally conducted off the coast anywhere from Lancelin down to Fremantle. We jumped in day and night, summer and winter and were only restricted by the prevailing weather conditions.'

The dangers of accident and fatality were ever present. But that only added to the excitement. 'We had so many adventures, so many funny stories and some near misses too,' he says. 'I recall a jump I did at Toogoolawah in Queensland in 1986. It was the army national championships and I was participating in the accuracy competition. The idea was to land on a small cushion which had an electronic pad on it which recorded distance from the centre. Obviously the closest to the centre over a number of jumps was the winner.

'The week or two previous to the competition, there had been quite a bit of rainfall in the area and the ground around the landing pit was quite soft. As a relative novice, I made a rather radical approach to the pit and at about

50 feet realised that I was going to miss the pad, so I made a bold correction which swung my body horizontal to the ground and planted my face firmly into the soft ground, leaving an imprint of my mouth, nose and goggles where I landed. It hurt like hell and I was totally embarrassed, but I got straight up and carried on like nothing had happened. Funny now, but many people have done the same thing and it's killed them, because the parachutes are flying faster now, and the ground has been much harder – I was lucky.'

On occasions, he was permitted to use his own parachute. 'In those days, you had to get them certified and checked by military riggers to jump them on a military aircraft,' he says. 'I did all that but we were doing a demo jump for the regimental birthday. It was 1988, at Swanbourne. We went out at 8,000 feet and I had what they call a 'floating bunny tail'. The deployment system was a little rabbit's tail thing that was attached to the bridle line on the back of the parachute. It had become dislodged before I exited and instead of being down at the bottom, it had dislodged and was now floating higher up my back.

'I put my arm back and I couldn't get around to reach it. You're falling 120 miles an hour; you look down at the ground and it starts to come up at you. That's not good. The activation height was 2,500 feet, so, second attempt – nothing. I started hanging out and realised that I couldn't reach it. One grab, two grab, nothing there. I went through cutaway procedure and then at last straight into the reserve, and "Whoops," 1,500 feet in the saddle, so it was quite ... interesting.'

He was uninjured. 'In civilian jumps your reserve parachute is normally smaller than your main parachute, but in military parachutes they're exactly the same because it's a different application. In the military situation, you're carrying all your equipment and if you have a malfunction on your main parachute and have to discard it: the reserve parachute has to be able to carry the same load.

'So I landed at normal speed. I walked away.'

10

PUTTING DOWN ROOTS

Parachuting provided an exciting and satisfying antidote to the training routine. Palmer's expertise in the highly competitive SAS environment turned out to be a double-edged sword. When you stand out from the pack you attract enemies, particularly among men in a world where controlled aggression is a highly prized character trait. One incident in particular would have far-reaching effects.

'This bloke, a senior SASR member, had left the unit, gone away and come back promoted to warrant officer class 1,' Palmer says. 'He hadn't jumped for some time and had done very limited jumps on square parachutes. We did a demo jump, in which he participated.'

They took off, and when they jumped Palmer was first to land. 'I landed right on the target,' he says, 'and we were all standing as a group watching him come down. He misjudged the landing approach. Even though he saw us land into the wind, he came in crosswind hard and fast, and when he hit he somersaulted across the grass. He got up and it was one of those things that looked so funny you can't help yourself. As he looked over, I'm laughing my head off at him. We were all laughing but he looked at me and suddenly I was getting a cat's ass stare.'

'From that point on he had it in for me,' he says. 'The next thing there was an incident up at the soldiers' boozer one night. I didn't even know it had occurred until after the event. The incident was on one side of the building and I was on the other side. There had been a fight and the duty officer got involved. I was grilled and according to the authorities I should have stopped it. I was a senior person there and I should have seen it coming.'

It was an obvious move, Palmer says, to get another bad mark against his name. 'In the next incident efforts were made to remove me from the regiment with a preconceived plan of attack which backfired on him,' he says.

Once again, the parachuting provided a useful outlet for the pressures within. Clint was in a team that travelled to Exmouth Gulf to continue training. To minimise risk from both sharks and drowning, the regiment always had boats in the water near the landing zone. (Standard Army practice which covers the SAS as well as every other unit.)

'The risk management necessitates that you have to have personal flotation devices when you jump into water,' he says, 'and the number of safety craft depends on the weather conditions and the experience of the jumpers. For novices, you have one boat per person; on a flat, calm day with experienced jumpers, you get one safety craft per three people.'

On this occasion Palmer was first out of the aircraft. 'Fundamentally, there's no difference to a water jump than there is to a land-based jump except for the landing, and so to set up for a landing in water, you have to prepare yourself slightly differently. The impact with the surface of the water is significantly less than the impact on the hard ground. Although sometimes landing on soft ground is better than landing on water, depending on how fast the wind is blowing. On land they'd call the jump off, whereas you're allowed a bit more leniency with wind strength landing on water.

'On impact, you go under the water and you're basically getting dragged down,' he says. 'So when you hit the water, you disengage one of the risers so the parachute collapses. But you only let go one riser so that the canopy is still connected to the harness, and is not lost.'

He was on a steerable parachute, so manoeuvred to land near one of the boats. However, to his astonishment when he hit the water it was just below knee deep. 'It was quite funny really,' he says. 'A little splash and I stood up, took about 20 paces and I was back on the beach. I didn't even get wet. I could have probably turned a little bit earlier and landed deeper out but I didn't anticipate the water to be so shallow. Normally it drops away quickly about 20 metres out. And as well I had to face into the wind on impact.'

The time would come when Palmer was instructing his regimental mates in the full range of parachute jumping. From the beginning he was a stickler for 'the book'. 'The regiment doesn't take shortcuts,' he says. 'We follow the guidelines that Defence has laid down because experience has shown us over time that if we go outside them it's a recipe for disaster. And the ramifications when things go wrong are monumental. So we're no different from any other parachute unit in the Defence Force.

'However, there is the ability within Special Operations Command to conduct realistic training – that means as close as possible to the real thing without breaking the rules, without taking unnecessary shortcuts, and without endangering the participants. It's a matter of doing things as safely as possible within the constraints of the environment in which you're working.

'I know that sometimes people have this misconception that SAS blokes go out there and they do it harder, tougher, stronger, and they're a bunch of cowboys, break the rules, do what they want. Well, it's not true. The bit that's true is they're harder, tougher, stronger, but they're far more professional in their approach to things and they're well versed, well trained and extremely professional in their attitude. That's the difference.' They even learn to pack their own parachutes. 'We have a bit more versatility or flexibility that way,' he says.

However, parachuting is an intrinsically hazardous endeavour, and despite best intentions fatalities have occurred. 'There have been a number of them,' he says. 'I was in the unit when one of our fellows was killed. It was a training exercise. He was a "chook" and had just finished his free-fall course. We were doing a demonstration jump for the remuneration tribunal who were visiting Perth, and they were actually watching the rehearsal for the next day. This guy jumped out and had difficulties under canopy and floated off into the forest. His equipment apparently shifted in the opening process, wrapped around his neck and was obviously restricting him. He couldn't clear his airways because when he floated off in the wilderness he was already unconscious and he was probably dead shortly after that. We found him hanging in a tree.

'They all witnessed the jump and saw him go in and realised how dangerous it was. They gave us more money. It was tragic but pretty convenient at the same time, from a callous point of view.'

The seemingly endless training regime continued. However, a new and exciting element had entered his private life. In the summer of 1986–87, he had visited the Commonwealth Bank in a Perth shopping centre with his father, who, with

Isabel, had by now retired to the Perth suburb of Craigie. Clint knew one of the tellers there, Debbie Price, the wife of a work colleague. And as he struck up a conversation with her he suddenly became aware of a beautiful young woman at another counter.

'She had permed blonde hair with a red ribbon tied in it,' he says. 'She looked absolutely stunning and I couldn't keep my eyes off her. As much as I tried to maintain conversation with Debbie, I was excited at the fact that this beautiful woman was paying some attention to me!

'I left the bank that day wondering about the possibilities and knowing that I would like to see more of her. At the earliest opportunity I contacted Debbie and asked her who this woman was and what were her circumstances.'

He made contact, and arranged to meet her at the beer garden behind the Cottesloe Hotel, overlooking Perth's most picturesque beach. 'It was a typical summer afternoon in Perth,' he says. 'Warm sunshine and a friendly crowd. The Cottesloe Hotel beer garden was a favourite haunt for many young people to spend a Sunday afternoon socialising before the working week ahead.

'Kimalee had such an impact on me that although I had told her I wasn't interested in settling down or being a husband, I soon realised that it wouldn't be long before I'd change my mind.' And it seemed that his feelings were reciprocated. 'At that time I was out and about with the boys quite often', he says, 'but it seemed that every time I turned around Kimalee was standing there looking at me. Mind you, it was extremely hard to resist a pretty face with her head tilted sideways sporting that questioning look. So like most good men I succumbed to the fairer sex and agreed to hook up and plan a future together.'

In May 1989, they moved into his parents' house in Craigie and applied to the army for de facto status. 'It was at 104 Craigie Drive that I asked Kimalee to be my wife,' he says. 'On 8 June 1989 I said to her, "What do you reckon about getting married? I think we should, don't you?" The response was, "Are you asking me to marry you?" It took me a second or two, then I said "Yes." She also said yes, and the rest, as they say, is history.'

However, all was not smooth sailing. Palmer himself was having problems with his interactions. 'I had an incident in 1989 where I punched a captain, and that put a bit of a dampener on things,' he says. 'It happened on a CT course at a Victorian Air Force base. He was being obnoxious. The army encourages controlled aggression but I got to the point where I thought this guy's just not getting it so after a number of warnings he didn't listen so I went "whack". There's no excuse; I should have just walked away. I tried to but this guy would follow me, literally, and keep antagonising. I don't know what his beef was. He was very bad on the alcohol.

He had a history of bad behaviour when he was on the piss . . . so, third strike and you're out.

'As soon as the incident took place, I told Kimalee and discussed it with her. I went to my immediate superior straight away and told them what happened. They said, "Ah! Forget it." At that time there was no action taken. And the guy I hit approached me two days later and he said it was his fault; he apologised and [said] he would take no further action. I was happy with that until two and a half months later in the mess some of the young captains were talking about him and the incident. The commanding officer happened to be in the mess and overheard the talk and said, "We'd better investigate this", and I was charged with assaulting a superior officer. He faced three counts of assault on me. He was asked to show cause and didn't satisfy the hierarchy so was asked to leave the army. Poor bastard!

'I was reduced in rank and basically it put me back two years. I was about to be promoted to sergeant when the incident occurred. So I was put back to lance corporal and it took six months to get back to corporal and two years to make sergeant.'

By October he had secured a married quarter at Swanbourne. 'The wedding was a simple affair,' he says. 'We were married by a civil celebrant at Harold Bowers Gardens in Perth on 23 December 1990. Around 80 guests, including family, were invited and we held our reception at the Gratwick

Club at Campbell barracks. It was the first function in the newly completed extensions to the club.

'The following morning we headed off on our honeymoon', he says. 'At about six o'clock in the morning we drove out and headed north to Coral Bay, where we spent the next week living in a tent and enjoying the sunshine and clear cool waters of the north-west.

'As the years passed, and the children came along, many of our priorities were rearranged as the children and the family always came first.'

In August 1991, Clint was on hand for the birth of their first child, Callan, at the St John of God Hospital in Subiaco.

'His birth was an eye-opener for me,' Clint says. 'It was a relatively short labour at only two hours but the event was not without tension because the doctor who was going to deliver the baby was half an hour late. Callan was born quite blue; he had his umbilical cord around his neck and it was some time before he got a good supply of oxygen. There were a few anxious moments because he wasn't responding initially, but he recovered quite well.'

After a few days they returned to the married quarters in Alamein Crescent. 'Kimalee was an excellent mother,' he says. 'She knew exactly what she wanted. She set the house up and spent a lot of time creating a practical and functional family home. There were, however, times when we had to pack up house and move, which is the most stressful thing a woman can experience next to childbirth – or so they say! As part of the upgrade of Defence housing, we went from 78 Alamein to 63 Crete, then on Christmas Eve 1992 we took the keys for 12 Coast Rise, the very first of the new homes in stage one of the redevelopment.

'It was all very nice – brand new home. I was very proud and my thoughts were of raising a family, being a dad.'

On the surface, they were the ideal family.

11

OFF COURSE

Jim Wallace was succeeded in December 1990 by Lieutenant Colonel Duncan Lewis, 37, who had joined the regiment in 1977 two years after graduation from Duntroon. In 1982, he was a UN observer in the Middle East and was in Lebanon during the Israeli invasion. Since then he had commanded the SAS base squadron and 2 Squadron, and risen to second-in-command of the regiment.

Duncan Lewis's experience in the Middle East was no coincidence. Australia's major ally, the United States, was realigning its foreign policy priorities in that region. During his tour as CO, the US prosecuted the first Gulf War – Operation Desert Storm – under President George H. W. Bush in 1990–91. And while the SASR was not involved in any combat operations, the military focus extended to that region. In June 1991, the regiment provided support personnel to a mission – Operation Habitat – in Turkey and Northern Iraq to assist Kurdish refugees who had been driven north by Saddam Hussein's forces.

After the war the SAS was represented for the next nine years in the UN teams to oversee the destruction of Iraq's weaponry, including the Weapons of Mass Destruction that were to become the major public justification for the 'pre-emptive' war orchestrated by Bush's son George W. and his Vice-President Dick Cheney. The regiment would be well placed to provide independent intelligence on the existence or otherwise of these WMDs.

The SAS was also involved in North Africa when a UN force was established in 1991 to monitor the ceasefire between contending Moroccan groups in the Western Sahara until a referendum could be held. This exercise would continue until 1994 when the UN withdrew. By then the referendum had been abandoned. And while the status of the Western Sahara territories remains unresolved, protests in the 2012 Arab Spring did bring a measure of democracy to the Moroccan kingdom.

There was also some SAS activity in Australia's strategic region with the deployment of several Sabre squadron operators, together with communications experts, in the UN's Cambodian mission in the early 1990s. SAS signallers were stationed in the more remote locations, where all their training was put to the test in tours that lasted from seven to 13 months.

However, these were all UN missions. It was not until 1994, under a new CO, Lieutenant Colonel Don Higgins, a Duntroon classmate of his predecessor, that the regiment was able to conduct an independent operation – the first since the Vietnam War 23 years previously. It had its genesis two years earlier when the UN intervened in Somalia after civil war there led to mass starvation and anarchy. A group from Australia's 1st Battalion RAR was part of a security operation, and shortly after it was withdrawn in 1993, a US Special Forces contingent was caught up in the infamous Black Hawk Down tragedy that saw 18 of their number killed and dismembered. President Bill Clinton immediately withdrew all American forces.

Sixty-seven Australian aid workers from the Australian Services Contingent (ASC) had been under US protection and the call went out to the SAS to replace the Americans. Ten members of 3 Squadron with special skills in free-fall, water operations and communications were assembled under the command of Sergeant Gary Kingston. Known as J Troop, the unit underwent last-minute training and briefings at Campbell Barracks and a two-man advance party led by Sergeant Malcolm Wood left by civilian aircraft for Mogadishu on 31 March. The remainder arrived in the Somali capital on 14 April 1994.

The ASC worked from two main locations – a camp at the Mogadishu airfield and the Australian Embassy (Anzac House) in the city, 3 kilometres away. J Troop's task was to protect ASC personnel in the field; provide them with weapons training; develop an evacuation plan; and support them with emergency medical aid and communications. They employed UN armoured personnel carriers as well as their own Land Cruisers and utes. They were fully armed with pistols, rifles, light machine-guns and M79 grenade launchers; and they patrolled with body armour and NVGs for night operations. They established their own operating base at the airport, which quickly became known as Camp Gerbil after the small rodents that infested the area.

Three days after they arrived, a firefight resulted in the death of two Gurkhas and one Pakistani when the Nepalese camp took rocket fire from Somali clans. The Australian team nearby remained casualty free, and when the ASC was replaced by a second Australian group they were on hand to protect their entry. As they landed, one aid member reported, 'They positioned themselves around the aircraft in such a manner that at any given moment should an attack occur there were three overlapping arcs of fire that could have been returned.'[17]

The SAS unit had to use all the negotiating and discretionary skills from their training at Swanbourne. Sergeant Kingston says, '[We] came face to face with all types of armed men. [The troopers] relied heavily on their training in identifying hostile action and the use of appropriate counter-measures ... Other contingents often took casualties. On many occasions J Troop diplomacy prevailed, and the troop took a step backwards if they were completely outgunned and had no back-up.'[18]

However, armed confrontation was inevitable and was not long coming.

In May, a Canadian civilian helicopter went down 20 kilo-metres from Mogadishu and an armed mob threatened a replay of the Black Hawk Down tragedy. The Pakistani quick reaction force failed to respond and the Australians stepped into the breach. Eight SAS operators (by then known as 'Gerbils') took a chopper to the crash scene with doors closed. When they landed they flung open the doors to reveal a fully armed Special Force with weapons primed for action. The Somali gunmen in the crowd chose flight before fight and melted away. The Australians then turned their attention to youngsters in medical need and the tension quickly dissipated. The Canadian aircrew returned with them to HQ.

In the chaos of a lawless community sporting an arsenal of weaponry, the 'Gerbils' were constantly under threat of ambush and sniper fire. The Somali gangs attacked each other and UN personnel alike, and on 10 July they bailed up a three-vehicle UN convoy involving Malaysian, New Zealand and Italian personnel. The convoy commander surrendered to the gunmen and all were bashed and threatened with execution. They were released only after painful negotiations with the local warlords.

This put the SAS operators on high alert. When the Pakistani unit again failed to respond to a UN order to escort a convoy to the airport, the Australians once again took up the slack. And they were determined that they would not suffer the same fate. As the convoy approached the airport they were confronted by a Somali vehicle coming towards them with a gunman standing in the back aiming an AK-47 in their direction. One of the SAS NCOs, Gary Porter, raised his light machine-gun to cover the gunman, who responded by taking aim at the Australian. Porter fired first. The gunman and another Somali were killed instantly. The convoy kept moving. The Somalis faded into the distance. Thereafter, according to Kingston, the Somalis 'openly turned their weapons away from Australian convoys'.[19]

The government withdrew the ASC in November 1994 and the 'Gerbils' returned to Swanbourne at the same time, their work highly commended by the headquarters command. By then, another small group from the regiment had taken up station in Rwanda, providing medical support for the UN assistance mission there. Their tour was relatively benign. But their six-man successors in 1995 were caught up in the horror of the Tutsi massacre of at least 4,000 Hutu refugees at the Kibeho camp.

The Australians, under Sergeant Major Rod Scott, were particularly distressed because they were under strict UN orders not to open fire to protect the refugees. Scott said later, 'It is hoped that our soldiers never witness such obscenities ever again.' Despite the deployment of an Australian Army psychology team to the area to counsel the soldiers, the horror was indelibly imprinted on their minds.

All of these missions were carried out in the public eye.

Palmer was chosen to be among a select group that would have operated independently in Cambodia. 'The Australian Government was most reluctant to have splashed all over the tabloids, "SAS Deployed to Cambodia" because the question would be asked, "Why are we sending SAS troops to a UN mission?"' he says. 'That was one of the little let-downs in my career because when I was in 1 Squadron we were on notice to train up and deploy to Cambodia. It was the end of the Pol Pot regime and the UN had come in and taken over the establishment of a new government. So we were training up and training up, and then we got the official decision that the SAS weren't going.'

It was in the wake of one of these disappointments that Clint Palmer had a second serious fall from grace. It occurred in 1994 within the exchange program, Exercise Long Look, which the SASR maintains with the British 22 SAS Regiment. It includes senior British operatives observing specialised courses in Australia such as assault insertions and demolitions. On this occasion Palmer was given the task of chaperoning a British SAS sergeant through an introduction to service activity, where exercises involving aerial delivery systems were in progress.

It came at an unfortunate time for his family life. In January Kimalee had given birth to their second child, a daughter. 'Kelsee Morganne was an engineered baby,' Clint says. Kimalee really wanted a daughter and I was happy with that too – a boy and a girl – and she read a couple of books on the process to enhance the probability of conceiving a girl. And we went through the motions of this process for some time. I would get a phone call: 'Get home quick. Now!' So I would jump on my pushbike and ride like a madman, race home and be expected to perform. It was only 600 metres but "now" is now. So I call Kelsee our immaculate conception – as well as "my beautiful baby girl".'

Shortly afterwards, he and his British visitor had to leave Perth. 'We went across to the parachute school [at Nowra] to do some high-altitude training and operating a new parachute system with an automatic opening device and a GPS attached,' he says. 'You'd throw it out of the plane and it would automatically open and fly under GPS to a certain location. It had the capacity to carry up to a ton of payload.' This was meat and drink to the parachute expert. 'We worked on it during the week and at the weekend we went out and had a few beers. 'But then my guy got tangled up with this woman,' he says.

The Brit was determined to take the woman home to far-off Bomaderry. Palmer, who had also had his share of beers, was in a quandary. 'It was miles away,' he says. 'I remembered the boss saying to me before we went away, "Make sure you take care of this guy and look after him. Keep him out of trouble." Then, as he left with this girl, he got into a fight and I had to break it up. But he was determined to go with her so I said, "All right, I'll go with you." So off we went, back to her house, and I slept on the couch out in the lounge room. When I woke up it was 6 a.m. and we had to be back at work at 7.30.'

The Australian shouted at his charge to wake up. 'The girl appeared from the bedroom and I said, "Can you arrange a cab?" She says, "I don't have a phone." So where's the nearest one? "Oh, down the road about a kilometre there's a phone box."

'So I'm off down the road, running all the way. Rang a cab, ran back to the house and the cab finally arrived. We got to work and we're late. The boss says, "Where have you been?" and I told him the story. But we're reeking of alcohol and I copped it. I was pissed off because in my mind I was trying to do the right thing by this guy and got caught up in it. What would it have looked like if I'd said, "Okay, off you go, do your own thing," and I got back in time and they said, "Where's X?" I was between a rock and a hard place.

'Then a report of the incident reached Swanbourne and he didn't like it.' That was putting it mildly. His OC transferred Palmer from his Sabre squadron to the much less prestigious Operations Support Squadron, where they trained new recruits and ran courses. 'I was really pissed off after that,' he says. 'I suppose it could have been worse. But those are the ruminations in retrospect. At the time, it seemed to add to his feeling that he was hard done by.

However, once again he found consolation in his parachuting specialty. Among the more spectacular of his free-fall adventures took place during a trip to New Zealand in 1996 for Exercise Tasman Canopy, a bilateral operation between the parachute schools of Australia and New Zealand. Every alternate year, one would visit the other in order to maintain a core knowledge base at both institutions. The exercise normally took two weeks, and when the Kiwis were in Australia they would be taken to various locations to jump as well as jumping at the school itself. When the Aussies went to New Zealand, jumps were conducted on both North and South Island.

They had already completed a number of jumps at Auckland and Rotorua, 'and had flown to Christchurch to do a jump into the domain in the city and after that at nearby Burnham camp. The jump into the domain was done with a single pass with a split, seven jumpers per split, a total of 14 canopies in the air. He was in the second split and they exited the aircraft without incident.

'All parachutes opened successfully and we were transiting back to the drop zone,' he says, 'when I saw a parachute in front of me suddenly dip into a right-hand spiralled turn. I had very little time to react and knew immediately that there was going to be a collision. His body passed directly under mine, but his parachute hit centrally up my suspension lines, the impact causing his parachute to wrap completely around my lines, and at the same time my parachute also collapsed.

'During the collision I'd passed through his suspension lines and now his parachute had slid down and was wrapped around my body. I had no vision, as my face was completely wrapped in nylon material. As both parachutes collapsed, there was that horrible sinking feeling in my belly as we fell towards the earth. It was at that time when I literally saw the faces of my two children appear before my very eyes. The clarity and detail in their faces is something that will stay with me forever – I knew that I was going to die.

'A second or two later my parachute reinflated, which put even more pressure on my face because now he was hanging below me suspended under the weight of my parachute and his canopy still wrapped around my body. I quickly removed the cloth from my face enough to see where we were going and realised that I had no ability to steer the parachute. At this time we were 700 or 800 feet above the freeway leading into Christchurch. I was able to manoeuvre the parachute by pulling on the rear risers enough to find an opening in the trees and bring us both back onto the drop zone.

'We were going downwind, so we had the speed of the parachute and the speed of the wind behind us pushing us into the ground. The landing was horrific. The guy hanging below me hit the ground very hard and bounced a number of times before coming to rest. I tucked everything in and executed a parachute landing roll the best way I could to minimise any damage. As it turned out, I sprang to my feet and walked away, which is more than I can say for the young officer. He was in the hurt locker big time and was evacuated to the local hospital for observation over the next 24 hours.

'As fortune has it, the New Zealand cricket team was conducting a final training session on the adjacent grounds from the drop zone. A local television station was filming the Black Caps at their training. When the parachute collision occurred, one of the TV crew noticed it and immediately the cameras were on us all the way to the ground. The opportunity for a big story in the news that night was too much to pass, so the TV crew pursued us for the rest of the day trying to get an interview out of me.

'I declined, but a spokesperson for the Australian contingent gave an interview, and as well as the footage of the collision was screened on New Zealand national television that night. It also reached the West Coast of the US, Japan, the Philippines and the east coast of Australia. One of the Aussies who was in the first split of the jump also filmed the incident, including a close-up of the landing. When I saw that footage I wondered how the other guy came out of it so well. All I could think of was more unnecessary attention being drawn to myself at the time. 'We left the area and repacked our parachutes to conduct the next jump at the local New Zealand Air Force Base.' They did one more, but then the wind came up above jump limits, so they packed up and went home. 'By the time we arrived back at camp I was feeling like a truck hit me,' he says. 'A couple of beers and a good night's sleep saw me fit and raring to go next morning. Again I had been lucky.'

12
MOVING TARGET

By 1996 Jim Wallace had been promoted to full colonel and was stationed in Canberra as the commander of Special Forces. The government had recently released a Defence White Paper that envisioned a greater involvement in South-East Asia, and Wallace asked the regiment's CO, Lieutenant Colonel Mike Silverstone, to make a full review of its capacity to meet any new regional demands.

Silverstone, another Portsea graduate, had spent 18 months training in Britain with 22 SAS and the Special Boat Squadron. Earlier in his SASR career he had been a DS during Clint Palmer's aborted 1983 attempt at selection. He had been unimpressed with the medical diagnosis of his cold-induced asthma. 'He tried to sack me,' Clint says, 'but

I think he was just playing tough guy. When he was CO we saw eye to eye.'

He immediately established a team of majors, led by the operations officer Keith Perrimen, to begin the review. It would test the organisational and training arrangements to discover what changes might be required to prepare the regiment for the full range of regional operations, from counter-terrorism to specialised cooperation with Special Forces units.

It quickly became clear that, while the SASR was actively engaged with some regional forces – notably Thailand, Malaysia, Brunei, the Philippines, Indonesia and Singapore – there were serious blind spots, not least in Papua New Guinea, where Australia had special responsibilities from its colonial past. The SAS had been prohibited from training there following the outbreak of the Bougainville conflict in 1989. There was also a clear need to strengthen relations with other domestic Special Forces and supporting units, albeit that none of the others operated at such a demanding standard as the SASR. Indeed, there were particular concerns about the Army 5th Aviation Regiment, based in Townsville, which in 1989 had taken over the operations of the new Black Hawk helicopters from the RAAF and had since worked closely with the SAS.

Since 1990 they had carried out two training exercises a year, and by 1995 Silverstone was concerned about the degradation in aircrew skills and the maintenance of their aircraft. As a result of the review the 5th Aviation Regiment undertook an intensive refresher course for its pilots before the June 1996 exercise in the high-range training area near Townsville.

The exercise began well. But then on a night flight on 12 June, as six helicopters approached a target area, disaster struck. The three choppers in the lead were to insert their troopers directly on to the defended target. The fourth, flying immediately behind them, would carry a second wave of soldiers and the remaining two would supply covering fire from the air. The team had already practised the approach manoeuvre five times that day, but this time as they headed into the target the left forward aircraft suddenly veered right and smashed into the centre helicopter. One helicopter crashed to the ground and the 12 men aboard were killed instantly. Captain David Burke, pilot of the second helicopter, fought for control and managed to crash land. But immediately the aircraft burst into flames and, despite the heroic actions of SAS personnel on the ground who rushed to extract them, six troopers perished.

David Burke said later, 'There were rounds going off, there was ammunition flying in the air, there were explosions in the back of the aircraft, and these men, both SAS and air crew, were going into the flames and cutting people out and bringing them out.'[20]

Palmer was instructing on a locally run course at Swanbourne. 'We heard the news very soon after the crash but we had limited information,' he says. 'We pressed on with our night activity and of course the media reports kept coming. By the time we returned to Swanbourne it was midnight, and the full impact of the tragedy was known. Many of the wives and girlfriends had been brought into the Sergeants' Mess and were being comforted by unit members as their extended families in most cases were not available. My colleague running the course, Andy Miller, and I went straight to the mess and spent the rest of the night – until around 7.30 next morning – consoling these poor women.'

It was easily the most deadly incident in the regiment's history, and it followed four recent fatal training accidents in waterborne and free-fall exercises. The regiment was immediately placed under the most intense scrutiny, and this caused a wave of resentment from within. They were emotionally devastated at having lost so many good mates, yet it seemed they were being blamed for doing what was expected of them – operating at the limits of military capability to fit themselves for the most hazardous tasks conceivable in defending the nation.

The anger was exacerbated when the ADF High Command removed the regiment from its direct line of reporting to the military hierarchy in Canberra to the Sydney-based land commander. By now, former CO Don Higgins had moved up the chain to Command of Special Forces and his protests resulted in his own operation being moved to Sydney, where he too would be responsible to the land commander. However, he retained an additional capacity to report directly to the commander of the Australian Defence Forces in the capital if the situation warranted. The Special Forces Headquarters finally made the move in January 1998.

Coincidentally, Clint Palmer was also redeployed to Sydney at that time under orders from the new CO, Lieutenant Colonel Mike Hindmarsh, who had served as both a troop and squadron commander of the SAS. By then Clint had been promoted to warrant officer class 2 and in the new posting he would become CSM of 1 Commando Company. 1 Commando was a unit of the Army Reserve, and historically SAS operators, together with others with certain skills sets, acted as the nucleus of the administration. 'We conducted commando-type training,' he says. 'This involved aspects of special warfare: amphibious training, working with small boats – Zodiacs – specialist weapons training, roping, climbing, airplane rapelling from helicopters and parachuting; they were all part of the commando trade skill set.'

It was not a coveted posting. 1 Commando had never actually been deployed on operations, much less fired a shot in anger. They had been formed as a legacy of the independent companies such as Z Force in World War II. At the end of the war they were disbanded but, according to Palmer, the unit was part of the strategy of keeping a small, independently well-trained, deployable force 'in the back pocket' of Defence. They comprised 1 Commando Company with its resident headquarters in Mosman and 2 Commando Company in Fort Gellibrand, Melbourne.

Nor did he volunteer. 'I was quite happy to stay in Perth, continue in 1 Squadron and be promoted in situ,' he says, 'but I was told in no uncertain terms by the CO at the time that, "Clint, you have to leave. You have to do your time out in order to come back." It was a sideways movement. It created a space that I vacated for someone else to move into, and then when it was my turn to come back, someone else leaves and I come in. It's just a career progression thing.'

As CSM his role was to maintain discipline, lay down the law, and deal with any misdemeanours. 'You were responsible for the manning and making sure all the soldiers got on their appropriate training and promotion courses; also you had to see that all the positions in the unit were filled with the appropriately qualified people. So that was a big job. And I was also involved with keeping all the skill levels up to speed. I spent a lot of time at the ranges and doing basic skill-set activities such as navigation.'

But while it was a full-time task for the CSM, the reservists themselves came together for only three hours every Tuesday night and sometimes at weekends. In the peaceful 1990s, it was no simple task to retain their enthusiasm. 'This was specially the case in winter,' he says. 'When it's cold and rainy a lot of the guys don't turn up. However, if something sensitive was going down they'd be all over it.

'My boss [Major Peter Aswin] and I were discussing how we were going to maintain interest, and it turned out he was friends with one of the guys in the helicopter squad up in Townsville, and we knew that they were headed across to Perth to do some training over in Swanbourne. So he rang them up and said, "Hey guys, why don't you come via Sydney a couple of days early? And we'll play with you for two days because we need the choppers for training. It's an incentive thing for our guys to come in."

'The answer was, "Yep, no problem," so we advertised to the troops. We said, "Guys, hey, guess what? We've got Black Hawk helicopters coming for two days. Problem – it's Wednesday and Thursday." The reaction? "No worries, we'll be there", and so we had this list of 80 or 90 guys that were going to turn up on a Wednesday and another 70 or 80 on Thursday.'

Unfortunately, Murphy's Law intervened and the news came through that the helicopter squad had to stick to the original schedule. 'Well, on the preceding Tuesday night's parade,' Clint says, 'It was my job to let them know that the helicopters weren't coming. However, we were going to have a range practice that weekend and I expected all those 70 or 80 guys who were going to turn up for that chopper training to turn up on a Saturday or Sunday for the range. And three guys turned up!'

While the work could be frustrating, the job had its compensations. The Palmers were housed at Mosman, only 100 metres from the military compound at Sydney Harbour's Little Head where he worked. 'I was home every night except the odd weekend or a week when we went away,' he says. 'So my time at home with the family was better. We lived in an army house and Callan went to Mosman Primary.'

Kimalee had lived in Sydney before and didn't enjoy it at all. Clint says, 'It took me some convincing to get her to come in the first place. But after 12 months she wasn't happy – too far away from home, her family, her friends." Finally she said, "You're supposed to go back after two years anyway, so we'll go back now." I said I'd talk to the boss.'

The CO, Lieutenant Colonel John 'Radar' Kemp was understanding. 'He said he'd try to get married quarters allocated back at Perth so the family could go back ahead of time,' Clint says. 'And that's the way it worked out. My family was picked up, taken back to Perth into a married quarter, and for the second part of my posting I lived there [in Sydney] alone. I moved out of the house and had to find accommodation. Luckily at 1 Commando company we had transit accommodation at work – a demountable brand new bedroom, bathroom and a kitchen facility as well, so I lived there for 12 months. It was terrible.' They talked on the phone twice a week and he flew back to Perth a couple of times but then in July, with six months of the two-year posting to go, he was ordered to deploy to Bougainville.

Named after the French explorer who is also commemorated in the brightly flowering tropical plant, Bougainville Island is a province of Papua New Guinea, and during World War II was a vital RAAF base. American troops fought a decisive battle against the Japanese there, and after the war it was administered by Australia until PNG achieved independence in 1975.

In the early 1970s, the international miner Rio Tinto began an operation to extract the island's abundant copper and gold from the Panguna district. Disputes over the environmental impact and the distribution of royalties sparked a secessionist movement, and in 1976 rebels proclaimed the Republic of North Solomons. When the PNG Government refused recognition and ordered the PNGDF to put down the rebellion, the rebels formed the Bougainville Revolutionary Army (BRA) and the conflict quickly escalated into a civil war. The PNGDF retreated from permanent positions on Bougainville in 1990, but continued military action that would eventually claim more than 15,000 lives.

It ended in October 1997 after negotiations brokered by New Zealand secured a truce. The following month, Australians arrived on the island as part of the Truce Monitoring Group (TMG), and over the next four years numerous SAS officers and NCOs served in the TMG and the renamed 300-strong Peace Monitoring Group (PMG). By July 1999, when Clint arrived, the island was well on the road to peace. The final treaty would be signed the following year. But tension remained, and at any moment a gathering of villagers could turn violent. His principal role was to provide close-order protection for the PMG's commanding officer, Brigadier Simon Willis. Shortly after Clint's arrival, Willis was succeeded by another Australian, Brigadier Frank Roberts.

Headquarters were in the capital, Arawa, and while the CO was there Palmer was free to undertake other duties. 'When he went on tour around the place and when he had significant meetings the situation required extra presence,' he says. 'Then I would be there. I had a team trained up but they were on standby. In the meantime, I would accompany the commander on most of his travels. We got on very well. He was very easy to talk to and he was a good man.'

However, Palmer's task was complicated by the fact that the PMG was an 'unarmed' mission. 'That's what made it difficult,' he says, 'because if something went nasty, you had nothing but your body, yourself to use as a deterrent or a weapon.'

Fortunately, the CO was never attacked. 'It became quite heated at times,' he says. 'At a couple of meetings we were trying to negotiate a way forward between the faction teams like the BRA and the resistance on the island, trying to get them to agree on certain projects. When there wasn't any agreement, the commander put his foot down and gave his view. It threatened to get out of hand but then things calmed down.

'But in that part of the world, sometimes crowds become very agitated quickly. So it was best to get the leaders away from that environment into a neutral area, somewhere where it was benign and quite calm. But that wasn't always achievable, because as soon as there was movement the people were very suspicious and they would come flocking there and then we had to keep them away.'

Palmer lived at Loloho at the loading facility in tents underneath a huge silo where the copper had been stockpiled during mining operations. His tour lasted five months and was relatively incident-free. And while it was his first overseas posting, the timing meant that he missed out on a much more significant operation: East Timor. Brigadier Roberts told the ABC at the time that some of the military personnel wanted to join their units in Timor. 'It's a war zone,' he said. 'This is not a war zone. It's only natural that, at least for the initial period, that the focus will be on Timor. I think people accepted that here. I mean we've still got the support of the families and everybody back in Australia.'[21]

Palmer says, 'I was actually in line to go a lot earlier, but the boss changed his mind only a few days before I was due to go, and so I had to wait another 12 to 18 months before I went. Had I gone to Bougainville, originally, as planned, I would have been back home by 12 months, and when Timor came up I probably would have gone straight to Timor.'

Instead he returned to Swanbourne in December 1999. 'It was a reasonably happy reunion with Kimalee,' he says, 'though when I got home there was new furniture; there was a holiday booked to go to Bali and I didn't know about this until I arrived. What a nice homecoming surprise.'

Back at work he ran into trouble. 'I was earmarked to go back to Ops Support as the squadron sergeant major,' he says. 'But that didn't happen because the incoming OC didn't want me. We'd had clashes in the past.'

13

EAST TIMOR

While Palmer was sidelined in Bougainville, the regiment's focus had turned decisively to Indonesia, first as riots and demonstrations in Java and Sumatra threatened the safety of 10,000 Australians living there, then to the vexed issue of East Timor. The crisis in the tiny former Portuguese colony had arrived after 25 years of unrest since Indonesia invaded it – with Australia's tacit approval – in 1975. An independence movement, Falantil, supplied and encouraged by Portuguese elements and the Catholic Church, had coalesced into an effective guerrilla force. And when the ageing and corrupt Indonesian President Suharto was replaced in 1999 by the erratic B. J. Habibi, Indonesian control over the province began to waver.

The Australian prime minister John Howard publicly broke with Australia's long-standing support for Indonesian sovereignty over the East Timorese community and suggested they be given a vote to determine their future national status. To his surprise – and dismay – Habibi abruptly reversed three decades of Indonesian policy and accepted the suggestion. He went further – in May 1999 he announced that the referendum would be held only three months later, on 28 July.

The province quickly descended into violence as the Indonesian military who had invested heavily in the region, and their proxies, the locally recruited militias, clashed violently with the independence forces. On 11 June the United Nations Security Council intervened with the establishment of the UN Assistance Mission East Timor (UNAMET) to be responsible for the referendum. Clearly, Australia would be called upon to take a leading role within UNAMET, so the SAS was put on full alert. Lieutenant Colonel Tim McOwan had succeeded Mike Hindmarsh as CO and found himself deeply engaged with the East Timor crisis. McOwan, 42, a Duntroon graduate from country Victoria, had joined the regiment in 1981 and risen through the ranks. He'd also spent two years with the British 22 SAS. Anticipating a deployment to the crisis centre, in February he had asked his operations officer, Major Jim 'Taipan' Truscott to begin work on a contingency plan.

Truscott responded immediately. 'We built that plan over the next month and were ready for East Timor six months before we went in,' he says.[22] 3 Squadron, led by 34-year-old Major James McMahon, was designated the regiment's 'contingency' unit and at McOwan's direction they undertook a month of intensive language training – half in Bahasa Indonesia (the lingua franca of the community) and half Tetum, the native language of East Timor.

As militia violence increased, the UN decided to delay the vote until 30 August. Then at a pro-independence rally four days before the referendum, the militias attacked with firearms and machetes, killing five and wounding many others. The Australian Defence Minister John Moore announced that he had ordered the ADF to assist in the evacuation of personnel from East Timor, particularly the UN mission in the capital Dili. The action would be designated Operation Spitfire, and for the first time since Vietnam the SAS would emerge publicly as the spearhead of Australia's defensive armoury.

By now the unrest in Jakarta and other major cities had been controlled – at least temporarily – and there was no immediate need for the mammoth extraction that had first been feared. The regiment's attention was focused on East Timor ... apart, that is, from its other major responsibility: the 2000 Sydney Olympic Games. Planning for that operation had actually begun from the moment Sydney was awarded the Games in 1993. In fact, it was a CT operational practice run in Black Hawk choppers that resulted in the 1996 Townsville tragedy.

CT operators attended the Atlanta Olympics, and on their return they began developing the system that would counter chemical, biological or radiological threats to athletes and spectators. This would involve basing one of the CT squadrons in Sydney throughout the Games with a specially designed staging area at Holsworthy Barracks and nearby Luscombe airfield. They would also use the naval base HMAS *Waterhen* on Sydney Harbour for waterborne threats; and another forward operating base for the clandestine boarding of a moving ship. It was a massive operation and conducted totally beneath the public radar. It would all come together in September 2000.

Meantime, Lieutenant Colonel McOwan and his operational planners received orders from Canberra on 27 August 1999 to deploy immediately to RAAF base Tindall in the Northern Territory to prepare for the East Timor mission. At Tindall, 3 Squadron was housed in a big shed and Major McMahon joined his CO at base HQ. There McOwan had learned of his appointment as commander of a joint task force, incorporating RAAF units and two RAR rifle companies. They were charged with evacuating all Australian and UN personnel from East Timor. Major McMahon returned to his squadron and began an intensive training regime using C-130 transport aircraft and Black Hawk helicopters.

On 30 August, the East Timorese voted overwhelmingly for independence, and in a vicious reaction militia gangs ran riot day and night in the capital. Hundreds of fleeing East Timorese climbed the walls of the UN compound seeking safety. As tension rose, a series of high-level diplomatic cables and phone calls secured Indonesian permission for Australian aircraft to land at Dili and Baucau. On 6 September, McOwan himself flew in the first C-130 rescue flight to Dili accompanied by 46 3 Squadron operators. Four more C-130s followed, all with SAS soldiers aboard. Their mission was clear and concise: first secure the aircraft on the ground; marshal the UN staff and other refugees at the airport; check to see they were unarmed; then load them on to the aircraft for the flight back to Australia.

When they reached Dili, the city was ablaze. From the air they could see long convoys of trucks heading to the Indonesian border loaded with goods and furniture. And as the plane landed and the SAS men disembarked, automatic gunfire rippled around the airport perimeter. While the troopers took up defensive positions McOwan met with Brigadier Jim Molan, the Australian Defence Attaché from Jakarta and Colonel Ken Brownrigg, the army attaché at the Embassy. They introduced him to the Indonesia Special Forces captain in charge of security, who took McOwan on a tour of the airfield defences manned by Indonesian soldiers to ensure there would be no inadvertent territorial clashes.

'They were there to make sure that we did not go beyond the boundary of Komoro airfield,' McOwan says, 'and they told us what we could and couldn't do around the airfield.'[23] Soon the first refugees arrived and were loaded aboard the transports. Despite the excitement and tension, by day's end some 300 had been evacuated without incident.

At the same time, Major McMahon, with a contingent of eight SAS soldiers, had landed two C-130 transports further east at Baucau and begun to board UNAMET staff and a group of terrified refugees who were being harassed by hostile militia. The SAS soldiers moved in to protect them and the militia backed down.

The United Nations Security Council met and established a peace-keeping mission, the International Force East Timor (INTERFET); and on 15 September Australia accepted leadership, with Major-General Peter Cosgrove taking command. James McOwan would command the Special Operations component known as the Response Force. He was happy to be working with Cosgrove. 'From the military point of view, he's a very good commander,' he says, 'and is prepared to support you as well.'[24]

Cosgrove was not known as a particular fan of the SAS, whose members he habitually referred to as 'chicken stranglers', a sly reference to their capacity to live off the land. But throughout the Timor mission there was an effective and professional spirit of cooperation. McOwan proposed the SAS secure the air and sea entry points for the international force through a combination of military actions and negotiations with the Indonesian Army (TNI). Thereafter, they would become the 'commander's telescope' as they deployed through the province and would provide 'a trusted channel [of information] directly responsive to the commander'.[25] In addition, they would conduct raids to extract troublemakers, undertake close personal protection (CPP) for senior officers, and conduct search and rescue operations, as well as their traditional surveillance and reconnaissance missions. Cosgrove signed off on the plan, and became one of the first recipients of SAS protection.

On 19 September they accompanied Cosgrove to Dili for a meeting with the Indonesian commander, Major-General Kiki Syahnakri, to coordinate the arrival of the international force which had departed Darwin the day before in nine warships. The meeting went well and set the tone for the rest of the mission, at least at command level. McCowan's Response Force arrived at Komoro airport by C-130s the following day. Many of the SAS soldiers now spoke Bahasa fluently and they quickly made contact with the TNI soldiers around the airport, paving the way for further landings of RAR troops.

The SAS consolidated their position at the nearby heliport, and the following day welcomed the arrival of six Black Hawk helicopters. This allowed them to deploy to trouble spots throughout the province. They quickly went into action, rescuing a British journalist being attacked by the militia.

However, while they would be keeping a close eye on the 'enemy', it was equally important to secure the cooperation of the Falantil units that had operated from mountain hideouts in their 24-year guerrilla war. Only by keeping the two sides apart could they ensure the success of the peace-keeping effort. It would require all the tact, diplomacy and a firmness of purpose developed through years of training for just such a task.

McOwan attempted to engage the militia leader, Eurico Guterras, in the operation but he refused to deal with the Australian. He was more successful in making contract with the Falantil command, notably the chief of staff and deputy to the imprisoned Xanana Gusmão, Taur Matan Ruak. He discovered the rebel's whereabouts through intelligence sources in the East Timorese community in Darwin and set out for the camp near Uamori in a helicopter with a 30-man SAS escort.

The Timorese put up their weapons and the diminutive Ruak appeared, accompanied somewhat incongruously by an Australian woman, Margharita Tracanelli, who had been working with the prominent East Timorese activist José Ramos-Horta. However, she took little part in the meeting, which extended for several hours. Having made the breakthrough, McOwan followed up by sending Truscott back to spend several days with the guerrilla leader to consolidate the relationship. This would prove pivotal in gaining the human intelligence (humint) from Falantil sources across the region.

SAS patrols in liaison and communication teams (LTCs) were now able to fan out to Falantil cantonments and camps in the hills. Once established, they conducted medical clinics and supplied a flow of intelligence on war crime sites, militia activity and Indonesian troop movements in the border areas.

Independent SAS patrols confronted both TNI and militia groups on many occasions, but Cosgrove often proved unwilling to permit a decisive action against the militia. Nevertheless, when intelligence revealed a militia force on the rampage in the east, McOwan decided to try again. The militia had allegedly massacred a group of nuns and was bearing down on more than 2,000 East Timorese awaiting forced deportation to West Timor from the ancient port of Com. McOwan put his case, and this time Cosgrove agreed. McCowan gave the order, and as the sun set, a contingent of SAS soldiers hurried aboard three Black Hawks. They landed at last light several kilometres west of Com.

Led by Major McMahon, all were issued NVGs and personal radios that allowed them to stay in formation as they advanced along the coast to the port. They discovered the refugees in a compound by the wharf. McMahon spoke briefly to the East Timorese and gained the clear impression that the militia were infiltrated among them, so ordered his unit to withdraw to an area above the compound to observe. It was a good call. Barely an hour later, a group left the compound carrying machetes and swords. But still he held back, suspecting that this was a ruse designed to persuade the Australians the militia had departed.

Another hour passed, and this time the SAS observers saw between 20 and 30 armed militia leaving the compound and heading for a waiting truck. The SAS operators moved quietly down the hill to intercept them. When they were less than 20 metres away, the troopers levelled their flashlights and ordered them to raise their hands. Caught in the glare, the 24 militia hesitated only briefly before laying down their arms. The troopers collected 14 automatic weapons and a variety of slashing instruments, and held the men captive till first light when the Black Hawks returned. Then they released the Timorese from the compound and bundled the captives into the helicopters for the journey back to Dili.

The operation – a total success without a single shot fired – was an eye-opener for Cosgrove. Thereafter, he would employ the SAS on a range of independent operations, not least the seizure of Balibo, the site of the notorious killing of five Australian-based journalists during the Indonesian invasion of 1975.

Two SAS patrols inserted as pathfinders for 2 RAR which would seize the town. They rappelled from a Black Hawk into rough country, then sought a hilltop from which to observe Balibo. However, one radio operator had landed heavily and broken his leg. He was immediately evacuated and the others pressed on through a tangle of thick scrub and prepared a landing zone just before the infantry troops arrived.

Three days later McOwan mounted a 'brush and block' operation on the militia stronghold of Saui with four Black Hawks landing troops from 3 Squadron and other elements of his Special Force. They set up a roadblock and almost immediately exchanged fire with a bus full of escaping militias, killing two before the others surrendered. Another group advanced on the area in trucks and two Land Rovers. About 5 kilometres from the target the Land Rovers were suddenly hit by a blaze of small arms fire in a classic ambush. Corporal Hogno was shot in the shoulder and Ron Juric, the machine-gunner in the second vehicle, took bullets in the arm and leg. The soldiers immediately returned fire and spread out in the scrub heading for the enemy positions, while unit leader Captain Jon Hawkins radioed Major McMahon at the roadblock. McMahon drove immediately to the ambush site and oversaw the medivac of the two wounded soldiers to Dili.

Back in Saui the Response Force soon uncovered evidence of a massacre in the half-built cathedral. McMahon set up a defensive perimeter, which remained in place until joined by the 3rd Brigade, which arrived by sea. It was Australia's first amphibious operation since World War II. The SAS was well and truly back in the game.

14

POLITICS IN PLAY

Between 11 and 20 October, the Response Force conducted four more patrols but without exchanging fire. However, as the 'big army' of Cosgrove's INTERFET occupied larger areas of responsibility, this reduced the capacity of the SAS to operate independently. Moreover, the RAR forces were unwilling to delegate the more demanding and exciting tasks to others. They too had been trained in combat, and were anxious for the opportunities to prove themselves. It was an understandable reaction. Fortunately, the SAS had other strings to its bow and for much of the rest of the Timor engagement they reverted to 'hearts and minds' operations.

They set up first-aid posts in isolated towns and villages, treating everything from dental emergencies to broken limbs, malaria and even leprosy. Conditions were often extremely primitive, and the plight of children and the elderly took its toll on SAS personnel with young families and ageing parents of their own back in Australia. Indeed, according to SAS historian David Horner, 'While the raids received some publicity, the most important work was with the [Falantil] guerrillas and the extensive surveillance patrols. These relied on the training, initiative and discipline of NCOs and soldiers who received little acknowledgement for their excellent work.'[26]

The long-range surveillance patrols kept Cosgrove well informed of the trouble spots across the region. But after Indonesia formally granted East Timor independence on 19 October, resistance to his INTERFET mission progressively diminished. The militia either retreated across the border or reintegrated into the community, albeit uneasily.

The INTERFET deployment ended in February 2000 with the transfer of military command to the UN. The administration of East Timor was taken over by United Nations Transitional Administration in East Timor (UNTAET). By May 2002, more than 205,000 refugees had returned from West Timor and other parts of the Indonesian archipelago. East Timorese independence was formalised on 29 May 2002, with Xanana Gusmão sworn in as the country's first president.

Whether the tiny nation could remain a viable economic entity thereafter only history would record. However, the transition to nationhood was an unalloyed success story for the United Nations, Australia and the SAS.

The easing of pressure on SAS resources in East Timor meant that the regiment could devote itself wholeheartedly to the Olympics. Aside from national considerations, it was a valuable exercise for the regiment in raising its counter-terrorism capability to world's best practice. Designated Operation Gold, the responsibility for a trouble-free Games was placed squarely on the shoulders of 2 Squadron, which had continued its CT training throughout 1999 and the early months of 2000. However, it soon became clear that additional CT personnel were required to handle potential incidents in Canberra, Sydney and possibly overseas. So the structure of the operation was changed to create two separate task forces drawn from 2 Squadron and supplemented by elements from 3 Squadron on its return from East Timor.

Once again, the regiment would disappear beneath the public radar, and in March 2000 a Tactical Assault Group deployed secretly to Randwick barracks in Sydney for a month's training. They relocated to Swanbourne to analyse the lessons learned then returned in May for a series of five major exercises in and around the city. These included a dangerous boarding of a ship under way for which they used the navy's amphibious workhorse, HMAS *Manoora*; and a siege hostage operation at the Olympic baseball stadium.

The Olympics exercise also brought the regiment into close contact with Prime Minister John Howard, an association valued by both sides but which would have unfortunate consequences for the SAS. Since its inception, the SASR had found itself under fire from several military and political directions, so welcomed the opportunity to gain favour with the head of government. For his part, Howard, who held Special Forces operators in almost as much awe as Test cricketers, understood instinctively the political value of a personal relationship with the spearhead in Australia's military arsenal. So when a CT rehearsal was involved, the prime minister was more than happy to participate.

The Games security team also decided to go public with some of the more spectacular training exercises such as rappelling from helicopters onto Sydney's tall buildings, and this exposed the SAS in a way that added to their mystique. And when the Games scored the IOCs' award of 'the most successful ever', the SAS shared in the general approbation. By the end of 2000 the regiment was riding high.

Then came *Tampa*. By August 2001, Lieutenant Colonel 'Gus' Gilmore had succeeded McOwan as commanding officer. He had graduated from Duntroon in 1983 and risen through infantry and Special Forces appointments, commanding an SAS Troop in 1988 and subsequently as adjutant, operations officer and squadron commander.

In Canberra, Prime Minister John Howard was preparing for an election against a resurgent Labor Party under former Defence Minister Kim Beazley. The opinion polls put Howard in danger of defeat. However, on one highly emotive issue – the arrival of increasing numbers of refugees from the Middle East by boat – Labor was vulnerable.

At dawn on 24 August, the *Palapa 1*, a 20-metre wooden fishing boat with 369 men, 26 women and 43 children aboard – mostly Hazaras, a persecuted minority in Afghanistan – became stranded with engine trouble in international waters about 140 kilometres from Christmas Island. Two days later, Australia's Rescue Coordination Centre (RCC) in Canberra, which had been alerted by Coastwatch surveillance, requested all ships in the area to respond. The nearest was the Norwegian freighter MV *Tampa*, commanded by Captain Arne Rinnan, and he immediately changed course to rescue the passengers and crew. The RCC sent a plane to guide him to the stricken boat. The rescue operation transferring the passengers to the *Tampa* was completed in about four hours.

Christmas Island was the closest port, but since it didn't have the facilities to berth a ship of *Tampa*'s size, the Indonesian authorities agreed to its being sent to Merak on the west coast of Java. However, when the passengers learned they were headed for Indonesia, five asylum seekers confronted the captain on the bridge and demanded he take the vessel to Christmas Island. 'They behaved aggressively and told us to go to Australia,' he says. 'They said they had nothing to lose.'[27]

Rinnen again changed course and cabled the RCC seeking permission to unload his passengers at Christmas Island. His vessel was designed for its 27 crew, not 438 refugees, many in poor medical condition, he said. And since there were no lifeboats or other safety equipment aboard, this made it officially unseaworthy.

Howard escalated the issue politically by introducing a Border Protection Bill into the Parliament, saying, 'We decide who comes into this country and the circumstances in which they come.' Then, in an unprecedented move, he ordered the SAS to board the ship and force it to leave Australian territorial waters.

A fully armed SAS contingent under Major Vance Khan sped out to the *Tampa* and boarded her without incident. Footage of the dramatic operation was restricted to the departure of the SAS vessel from the shore. But for the next five days SAS medics and troopers remained aboard while negotiations took place between the Australian, Norwegian and Indonesian governments about the eventual fate of the refugees. And all the while Howard turned up the political temperature as Beazley vacillated then surrendered to the forces of exclusion. The refugees were finally transferred to HMAS *Manoora* and taken to a detention centre on Nauru as part of Howard's 'Pacific Solution'.

It is a tribute to the discipline and professionalism of the SASR that they were able to defuse a highly explosive situation on board, to assuage the fears of both the crew and the refugees in the most testing conditions.

However, there was widespread concern – both inside and outside the regiment – that they had allowed themselves to be used as political pawns. And indeed, during the election campaign Howard used every opportunity to exploit the divisions in the opposition on the issue. Beazley was pictured as weak on 'border protection' in sharp contrast to Howard's uncompromising stand, despite the fact that the overwhelming majority of the *Tampa* refugees were eventually resettled in Australia and New Zealand.

Howard's coalition government triumphed in the November election, and undoubtedly the *Tampa* affair was a significant factor.

However, it was not the only one. By then another event had changed the course of history. On 11 September two commercial aircraft had ploughed into the World Trade Towers in Manhattan; a third had smashed into the side of the Pentagon; and a fourth – targeted for the US Capitol – had crashed into a Pennsylvania field after a valiant struggle by the passengers. As it happened, Prime Minister Howard was in Washington at the time for meetings with US officials and the president, George W. Bush.

The pilots who had taken control of the doomed aircraft were fanatical agents of the terrorist organisation al-Qaeda, founded by the son of a Saudi Arabian billionaire. Born in March 1957, Osama bin Laden was raised as a devout Wahhabi Muslim. His father, Mohammed, died in 1967 in an air crash in Saudi Arabia when his American pilot misjudged a landing. His eldest half-brother, Salem bin Laden, the subsequent head of the bin Laden family, was killed in 1988 near San Antonio, Texas when he accidentally flew a plane into power lines.

Osama was educated in Saudi Arabia, where he attended university but was increasingly devoted to religious studies and left before completing an engineering degree. In 1979, he joined the Mujahideen in their fight against the Soviet invasion. He poured funding into the organisation, which had been founded in the 19th century to resist British rule in Afghanistan. He also recruited fighters from the Arab world, thus spreading his message on two fronts.

In 1988, he formed al-Qaeda as an instrument of the jihad in Islam's perennial struggle against the 'infidel' and in 1992 was banished from Saudi Arabia. He shifted his base to the Sudan, and when US pressure forced him out he established a new headquarters in Afghanistan, where he found common cause with the Taliban and formed an alliance with its leader, Mullah Mohammed Omar. From his Afghan redoubt he declared war on the United States and began a series of Embassy bombings on 7 August 1998, in which hundreds of people were killed in simultaneous truck bomb explosions in Tanzania and Kenya. The attacks were linked to local members of the Egyptian Islamic Jihad, but CIA and other intelligence sources clearly identified bin Laden as the prime mover in the operation.

The consequences for Australia would play themselves out over the next decade.

Meantime, back in Perth, throughout 2000 Clint Palmer remained in Demolitions Wing of the Operations Support Squadron, but combined it with Air Operations, where his parachuting expertise was highly valued. This included High Altitude Parachute Operations (HAPO). 'It's a skill which takes time and resources to become competent [at] and maintain,' he says. 'Most Special Forces units around the world have a HAPO capability, and we are up there with the best.'

The RAAF supplies the aircraft on HAPO exercises and places a height restriction of 25,000 feet above mean sea level, although in other countries the limit is raised to 35,000. The initial training regime is intense, and graduates must requalify every five years.

'Troops exit an aircraft at altitude, open their parachute and fly to a target area without the aircraft being detected from the ground,' Palmer says. 'The jumpers can free-fall to a pre-designated opening height, normally around 3,000 to 4,000 feet; or jumpers can exit the aircraft offset from a target, open the parachute and fly long distances to a predetermined landing zone.'

Either way, the jumps take a physical toll on the operators and they risk decompression illness similar to the bends among deep-sea divers. But the high altitude, high opening jumps are particularly taxing, as up to 35 minutes can be spent flying the parachute in sub-zero temperatures before landing.

'One jump we did at Woomera in South Australia was in the middle of winter,' Palmer says. 'We exited the aircraft at 25,000 feet at about three o'clock in the morning and the wind chill factor was significant enough to record minus 53 degrees when we left the aircraft. We opened after only a five-second delay and were sitting in the saddle at 24,000 feet, absolutely freezing. After 25 minutes under canopy, I remember landing and collapsing in pain because my fingers were suffering frost nip, and the reheat pain literally took my breath away. I don't think I've ever been as cold as that morning.

'A high-altitude, low-opening descent can be just as cold, but because of the speed you fall, you don't spend enough time at altitude to get cold,' he says. 'Having said that, above 15,000 feet it's still damn cold. Over the years I have done a lot of parachuting out of RAAF Base Learmonth near Exmouth in Western Australia.'

On one occasion, they exited the aircraft from 25,000 feet and approximately five nautical miles out to sea. The brief was to open at 20,000 feet and then fly across the peninsula back to the air base where the drop zone was located. On this jump they were fully laden with combat equipment, and the opening shock at that altitude snapped both of the steering lines on Palmer's parachute. It also dislodged one of the clips attached to his equipment, and his oxygen mask flew off the helmet. 'I recovered the oxygen mask as a priority,' he says, 'and then faced a dilemma of cutting away the main parachute and flying my reserve, or continuing on with the main parachute, which was fully inflated but not steerable.

'I decided on the latter and managed to track back to the drop zone landing only 200 metres short of the designated impact point. One of the other guys on that same jump was not so lucky. He encountered the same problem as I did on opening, but he didn't quite make it back and slammed into the walls of a steep canyon some 10 kilometres from the drop zone. We launched the search and rescue helicopter, and located him a little worse for wear about an hour later.'

In 2001, he took a transfer to become squadron sergeant major of the Logistics Support Squadron, an essential if unglamorous job that gave him a key supervising role in technical support, transport operators and maintenance personnel, cooks and catering, as well as the quartermaster sergeants.

While it was a vital administrative post, it was a far cry from the action, and at every opportunity he applied to return to a Sabre squadron. 'At that stage I was 43 years old,' he says, 'and the year before when the position came up for SSM of a Sabre squadron, they said "Well, you are 42."

'I said, "Don't you start the age thing, mate. I'm 42, so what?" The real story is that I just wasn't in the purple circle, so I didn't get the job for Sabre squadron SSM, which is probably the biggest let-down of my career. And it's because I'd been a bad boy a couple of years earlier and removed from my troop sergeant's position.'

Nevertheless, the rise of al-Qaeda that culminated in that 11 September attack would provide the SASR and Warrant Officer Palmer with a new and powerful raison d'être. The so-called 'war on terror' would make particular demands on the Special Forces of all Allied countries, not least Australia's.

15

AFGHANISTAN

John Howard's relationship with George W. Bush, built on the coincidence of Howard's presence in the US on 11 September and sustained by his devotion to the American alliance, meant there was never any question that Australian forces would be deployed to Afghanistan. And the SAS, with some associated RAAF assets, was his unit of choice for the job.

Palmer was determined to be part of it. And he was well placed to do so. 'I was at Operations Support Squadron and doing two jobs – sergeant major of both Demolitions and Air – waiting for my turn to go to Timor. This went on for 18 months or so, and I finally got notification that I was on the November rotation. September 11 happened just before I went on my RSM course. All our boys were out of Timor in October; November saw 1 Squadron deploy to the Middle East Area of Operations waiting to be called forward to Afghanistan. So while I missed Timor altogether, I was now waiting to see what was happening in Afghanistan.'

By now, former CO Duncan Lewis had been promoted to major-general and given charge of Special Operations Command. He had already developed a series of scenarios for Australia's Special Forces to respond to so-called 'asymmetric' conflicts in the Middle East. And the current CO, Gus Gilmore was chafing to get into the action. 'If it's going to be done, it's got to be done right,' he said. 'And we [had] earned the confidence of the Australian Government . . . that if they want something done, we'll do it right.'[28]

With the political and military commands pulling in the same direction, the Australian contingent was remarkably quick off the mark. RAAF Boeing 707 air-to-air refuelling aircraft with support personnel from 33 Squadron were soon operating from Manas Air Base in Kyrgyzstan. They refuelled Coalition aircraft in Afghan airspace while two AP-3C Orions flew maritime patrol missions in the Persian Gulf. The SAS was able to get boots on the ground in Afghanistan within two months.

The Australian mission was designated Operation Slipper, and as soon as he'd been fully briefed Gus Gilmore headed out with his operations officer Major Peter Tinley to the Middle East. His mission: to negotiate the role the SAS would play and the logistical arrangements that would allow them to deploy successfully. By 7 October they had joined with Australia's Ambassador to Saudi Arabia, Robert Tyson, a senior diplomat with strong ties to the international intelligence community.

A graduate of the Australian National University in History and Political Science, Tyson had formerly headed the Australian mission in Moscow and would later become Ambassador to Iraq. He spoke Arabic fluently, a vital asset in their dealings with the Government of Kuwait where they hoped to establish a base for at least 150 soldiers together with their vehicles and equipment. At the time, the US Combat Air Operations HQ in the Middle East was at Prince Sultan Air Base in Saudi Arabia, and Tyson was in the intelligence loop. So while the negotiations were complicated by diplomatic and trade deals – to say nothing of religious issues – the team secured the deal. There was one proviso: the Kuwaitis would sign off on the base but only if a third of the force remained there to defend Kuwaiti territory. It was a 'pain in the neck', according to an SAS operator stationed there later, 'but at least we had a base.' Moreover, it was within easy reach of the Americans' Camp Doha west of Kuwait City.

In a bureaucratic pincer movement, General Lewis also sent a small delegation – headed by Brigadier Ken Gillespie and including Major McMahon, seasoned by his Timor exploits – to the US Central Command in Florida. There they joined the team under General Tommy Franks planning the response to the al-Qaeda outrage. Franks's command extended over 25 countries, but the principal focus was on Afghanistan, where it had become clear that the ruling Taliban had provided sanctuary and support for bin Laden's terrorist operations.

Franks was a Texan, a 'big army' infanteer with virtually no experience of Special Forces operations. He had dropped out of college before enlisting, and finally gaining degrees under army programs. He worked his way up the ladder through administrative postings. His initial assignment as a general officer was as assistant division commander of the 1st Cavalry Division in the first Gulf War. In 1995, he was given command of the 2nd Infantry Division in Korea and two years later transferred to head the Third Army Forces Central Command in Atlanta. It was from this post that he was promoted to commander-in-chief of Central Command in Florida.

But while Franks had control of the big picture, Special Forces from around the world – Britain, Germany, Norway, France, Italy and Canada among others – were coming together to join the Americans in the anti-terrorist conflict centred in Afghanistan. All sought a significant piece of the action, and it was in this competitive environment that the SAS leadership sought to carve out Australia's role.

The professional and private friendships forged in Vietnam, and in subsequent joint exercises and personnel exchanges, paved the way for a ready acceptance at Special Forces level. And John Howard's ability to ingratiate himself with President Bush opened doors in the politico-military circles in Washington. However, the Americans were preoccupied with the battle on the ground in Afghanistan, where the Northern Alliance, supported by the CIA, was rolling up the Taliban forces and advancing through the major metropolitan centres towards Kabul.

It was not until Lieutenant Colonel Gilmore made personal contact with the US marine commander in US Maritime Central Command, Bahrain, Brigadier James Mattis, that they secured a well-defined role in the Afghan mission. Mattis was widely read and something of an Australia buff. The two men bonded immediately, and an elated Gilmore walked away with Mattis's brief ringing in his ears: 'What I'd like you to do, Gus, is to dislocate the Taliban that are in Kandahar at the moment. I want you to psychologically and physically dislocate them.'[29]

They would start at the first American forward operating base (FOB), Camp Rhino, about 100 kilometres south-west of Kandahar, the capital of the country under the Taliban government since 1994. It had been the Pashtun's traditional seat of power for the last 200 years. With a population of more than 500,000, it had been a magnet for terrorist groups such as al-Qaeda since the 1978 Marxist revolution. The insurgents also enjoyed the strong support of the official Pakistani spy network ISI.

Meantime, the SAS Squadron had been assembling its men and materiel in Kuwait and leased some Antonov aircraft, the giant transports developed in the Ukraine. They ferried a massive store of combat equipment and more than 20 of the all-important LRPVs – their specially modified six-wheel patrol vehicles – that would make the SAS a self-contained unit in the field. Once Gilmore was given the thumbs up from Mattis, they lost no time in making the move to Rhino.

The Americans were still assembling the basic infrastructure when the SAS arrived and established their own HQ in a corner of the base. Beyond fuel for their vehicles, their needs were few. They had brought rations for at least two weeks and ammunition for a series of patrols into 'tiger country', an expanding arc to the north-west with Kandahar as the principal objective. According to Gilmore, while the patrols were important in providing 'eyes-on' intelligence to the allies, they were vital in gaining the confidence of the American commanders who would decide how and where the unit would be deployed. And they were an outstanding success on both counts. 'Those first few weeks,' he said, 'really set up the operation in its entirety in Afghanistan for the Australian SAS.'[30]

Moreover, the regard was mutual. Mattis was a decisive leader and loyal to the men he commanded. Indeed, he took time out to write to Duncan Lewis that 'The conduct of your officers and men has earned them [our] full admiration . . . we Marines would happily storm Hell itself with your troops on our right flank.'

They patrolled ever closer to Kandahar, which was still in Taliban hands. And soon the Coalition had Australian eyes on the main routes in and out of the city. Then, in an audacious move never previously revealed, some SAS troopers disguised themselves as locals and infiltrated the city itself. The exact details of their actions are still subject to security restrictions, but time and again they had to use quick thinking and ingenuity to avoid exposure as 'infidels' while carrying out their mission of psychological and physical 'dislocation'.

Outside the city, the patrols went in search of Taliban and al-Qaeda training camps and village strongholds. By now it was December and Afghanistan's bitter winter disrupted patrols as the diesel fuel in the LRPVs froze, turned to sludge and choked the filters and cylinders. Other grades of fuel were tried but all failed, until they finally turned to a high-octane mix similar to aviation fuel. 'It did nothing for the engines,' says a trooper who was there, 'but it did solve the problem for us.'[31]

Back at Camp Rhino, the SAS was given the task of clearing a 30-kilometre zone around the perimeter. The operation was incident-free, and emphasised the confidence Mattis had in his Australian contingent. When the Americans moved in force on Kandahar in late December, the Australians were right behind them. They had bombed the city in October as US Special Forces and the CIA began operations around the country – in league with the Northern Alliance of warlords – to overthrow the Taliban. By the end of November, Kandahar was its last remaining stronghold, and was coming under increasing pressure. Nearly 3,000 tribal fighters under Gul Agha, the former governor of the province, attacked the city from the east and cut off the northern supply lines to the defenders.

Meanwhile, the airstrikes continued to pound Taliban positions inside the city, where the Taliban's supreme leader Mullah Omar was holed up. On 6 December, the US Government rejected any amnesty for Omar or any Taliban leaders, and the next day he slipped out of the city with a group of his hardcore loyalists on a convoy of motorcycles and moved north-west into the mountains of Uruzgan Province. On 21 December, the Gul Agha's forces moved into Kandahar while in a coordinated operation the US Marines took control of the airport and established a US base.

The Australians moved with the marines into their new base, where they celebrated Christmas in Afghanistan for the first time. There was hardly any mail as the RAAF didn't fly into Kandahar and since emails were banned for security reasons there was no psychological relief from the tension of combat. For while the Taliban administration had crumbled, the organisation remained intact and would soon reassert itself as a shadow government operating at the grassroots in opposition to the corrupt and distant government of the US puppet Hamid Karzai and the military 'infidels' occupying their land.

Back in Australia, Clint Palmer's extended posting at Swanbourne in the Operational Support Squadron then Logistics Support Squadron meant he was basically marking time. 'I think we just accepted life as it was; didn't have any real aspirations or goals at that time but to continue with the business of raising a family,' he says.

'I did one trip to the States to Fort Bragg in North Carolina and worked with the US Special Forces guys, mainly military, on demolitions. I also attended a military expo in Washington DC to look at any new gear and weapon systems to keep us up to date. It was huge, and took a week to see it all.'

Orders came through in January 2002 for his deployment to Afghanistan and once he arrived at Kandahar base he was almost totally cut off from the family. 'On that first trip,' he says, 'they weren't allowing us to talk back because it was a compartmentalised operation and you weren't telling other people what you were doing or where you were; that just wasn't on.

'We were allowed a 15-minute phone call per person for the whole deployment. The policy was comms lock-down most of the time. There were 100 blokes over there and one phone. I didn't bother writing. My mind set is, I'm the guy out there doing it hard; they're not, so I should be getting the mail; that's the way I think. They're probably thinking, you're away from us, why don't you write? I could have written, but it would be weeks and weeks before they got anything. And other than that, there was the security issue. So the relationship was strained.'

However the job at hand demanded a total dedication. The regiment's RSM had deployed initially to Kuwait together with the CO Gus Gilmore, but after a few weeks both men had to return to Australia to run the regiment. Lieutenant Colonel Rowan Tink was posted in Gilmore's place as task force commander with Palmer as the task force's sergeant major.

Tink came from a wealthy farming family in Southern NSW and was educated at exclusive Scotch College in Melbourne. He went directly from school to Duntroon and graduated in 1977 with a Bachelor of Arts (Military Studies) aged 22. He was posted to the infantry. 'I was asked to undertake an SAS selection course in 1980,' he says, 'and that was an extremely demanding few weeks, after which I was selected and had to return in November 1980, on posting to SAS. I then did two years in SAS before being posted to the US Navy SEALs in California.'[32]

Palmer says, 'Tink was my squadron commander in 1988. He had been to the US on a posting and came back with a whole lot of new ideas that the Yanks had taught him, and was making his mark by implementing these new ideas. Some were good,' Palmer says, but in his view, 'others didn't fit our scene.'

The SAS CO at the time, Lieutenant Colonel Mike Hindmarsh, was the initial commander of Pollard, a contingent of about 200 men deployed to Kuwait to provide warning and protection against an attack by Iraq's Saddam Hussein. However, two weeks after the Australians arrived, the UN Secretary General Kofi Annan negotiated a deal with Saddam and the pressure was off. Hindmarsh returned to Australia and Tink took over, and soon afterwards the force was being drawn down. The unit was withdrawn totally under a new commander in June. Tink's appointment to Afghanistan as head of the task force was a reprise of the earlier deployment, as once again he was taking over from the CO once the course had been set.

Palmer relished the chance to be involved at last in a combat mission. It was a big step up; the pressure was unremitting; and while he had a professional relationship with Tink, he says there was very little personal rapport between the two men.

Planning for Operation Anaconda was well advanced when the two replacements arrived in January following the failure of the American and Afghan forces to capture or kill the al-Qaeda leadership they had surrounded at Tora Bora on 17 December. The American Special Forces – known as Task Force Dagger – had left it to their Afghan allies to close out the battle and it was widely accepted that instead they had accepted bribes from the Taliban leaders to let them and their terrorist allies slip through the net.

In response the American High Command appointed 44-year-old Lieutenant Colonel Mark Rosenberg to take over as operations commander of Dagger. Known as a 'Fireball' and sporting a thick black moustache, Rosenberg had fought in Bosnia, Kosovo and Northern Iraq. He enjoyed the respect of his peers, and had the ability to motivate his men at the planning desk to work 18-hour days. He gave high-volume briefings with a red laser aiming device attached to his 9-millimetre Beretta pistol.[33]

The Dagger command worked closely with the CIA in pinpointing the Shahikot Valley as the key training ground and mountainous redoubt of the Taliban/al-Qaeda leadership. However, the operation soon had more arms than an octopus, as Navy SEALs, Delta Force units, TF 11, Advance Force

Operations (AFO) and others joined in, each as secretive as the next, and each bringing their own agenda to the table.

Despite the evidence from Tora Bora that relying on Afghan allies was a high-risk strategy in the Pashtun provinces, Rosenberg was determined to incorporate them into Anaconda. He believed that the valley contained at least 1,000 civilians among the Arabs, Uzbeks and other foreigners the Americans wanted to kill, and felt that only the local force could distinguish between the two groups. Moreover, he wanted the Afghans to 'own' the victory that he knew was coming. This led directly to the engagement of 'General' Zia Lodin and his ragtag band of peasant warriors – the 'hammer' on LaCamera's 'anvil'.

Once the overall strategy was accepted at Tommy Franks's Florida HQ, the military jigsaw began to assemble itself on 13 February under Field Commander 'Buster' Hagenbeck at the forward operating base at Bagram. And soon afterwards the Australians set out from Kandahar to report for action.

Clint Palmer, now 45, found himself roaring through a village outside the former Russian air base, heading for the range in preparation for the biggest Allied military action since Vietnam. The tension was building. Travelling by day in the cabin of an LRPV he says he was thinking ahead to the battle where he would be embedded with the front-line fighters, his first opportunity to distinguish himself in action in all his 18 years with the SAS. But then as they entered a village, suddenly at the side of the road he saw a young boy, looking straight at him, and he fancied he was his own 10-year-old son, Callan!

'I felt the shock of it go through me,' he says, 'I almost stopped, I wanted to go back; for a moment it was like he was there . . .' But then the moment passed and they were through. The vehicle picked up speed.

16

PEACE IN PNG

The vision of his son returned as the bullets started smashing into the rocks of Hell's Halfpipe. 'Again, when the mortars found their mark and were landing among us, the image of Callan by the roadside appeared with clarity,' he says. 'Oddly, the vision did not impair my real-time view of the surroundings. It was as though the flashes and images were superimposed. I could see them both clearly at the same time – a strange phenomenon.'

The memory was still fresh when he woke in fright the next morning in the great hangar at Bagram; but now the earth itself was moving and the roof above was swaying. The noise was unbelievable. He sat up. He was alone. He stood and began to run. When he made it outside all the occupants of the hangar were already out there watching as the earth tremors slowly subsided.

He'd been tucked away in a corner. No one had thought to wake him. And then the memory of his confrontation with Rowan Tink returned in force. That wasn't good.

'From the time I got back from Anaconda until I went home I avoided Tink, but worked with him on a professional level when needed,' he says. 'I knew I had to continue with the job until going home.'

Fortunately the posting lasted only a further month and both men returned to Australia. Palmer checked in at Swanbourne, then took some much needed leave. On his return to duty he resumed his role in the Logistics Support Squadron. Five months later he endured the prospect of decorations being awarded to his colleagues in Operation Slipper: CO Gus Gilmore – the Distinguished Service Cross; and his 'chook', Jock Wallace – the Australian Medal for Gallantry. As well, five other SAS personnel were decorated for their part in the mission at a ceremony on 27 November at Government House, Canberra. Rowan Tink later received an American decoration, the Bronze Star, for acts of meritorious service in a combat zone. Gus Gilmore also received the Bronze Star and the whole regiment received a Meritorious Unit Citation.

By then the mission was drawing down, and in December 2002 the SAS withdrew entirely. In Washington, President

George W. Bush, goaded by Vice-President Dick Cheney and a group of hardline foreign policy advisers, had turned his attention to a new target – Iraq – where the dictator Saddam Hussein ruled a disparate and mutually antagonistic population of Kurds, Shia and Sunni Muslims. Bush enjoyed the vigorous support of British Prime Minister Tony Blair, successor to the colonial rulers of former Mesopotamia who had created its arbitrary borders, and Australia's John Howard, dubbed by the US president his 'man of steel'.

In Afghanistan, the Americans passed responsibility to a much reduced International Security Assistance Force (ISAF) under the control of NATO, and shortly thereafter the Taliban and its fellow insurgents began to regroup. By now the former allies of Operation Enduring Freedom were preoccupied with building a case for a pre-emptive war against Saddam Hussein on the specious grounds that he had somehow been connected with al-Qaeda and possessed Weapons of Mass Destruction. Clearly, Iraq would be the next combat front for the SAS.

While the regiment made its preparations for a new Middle East deployment, Warrant Officer Clint Palmer was, in the immortal phrase of Sam Goldwyn, 'included out'. In fact, his next deployment could hardly have been further from the action in the Persian Gulf. 'That's when I left to go to New Guinea,' he says. But he'd been on the outside before and would ride it out. However, Palmer was also coming to terms with a more personal discovery delivered by his father, Terry, a revelation that went to the heart of his self-perception.

His mother, Isabel had died in 1987 at only 54, and Terry was now living alone at their Perth home. He sent an invitation to all seven children summoning them to a family conference. Inside each envelope was a letter that shocked his son to the marrow.

Written in Terry's copperplate script, it explained how he had attended the Australia Day concert in Perth's Entertainment Centre, which had begun with a performance from 'the Original Australians' that had led him to 'some soul-searching and personal stocktaking as a result of indisputable evidence of my own hybrid racial background!'

He was descended on his mother's side, he wrote, from an Aboriginal woman born in the Roma district of Queensland.

What had been a grey, uncertain doubt in my mind since ever I began remembering my earliest childhood has finally been cleared up, and I am totally at ease with the whole situation. You will each have to deal with this information in your own way, but at least you will never have any doubts about who you are, where you came from, and you were told by your father!

'I was pretty shocked,' Clint says. 'I asked him why he waited for so long before he told us, because to my way of thinking if you are who you are, why hide your heritage from your own children? There's got to be a reason why you did that, and it was his problem, his hang-up, his reasons. But it's not just about him. It's about the family.'

Until that moment, he says, there had never been a hint of an Aboriginal connection. But when he thought about growing up around Batchelor and mixing so easily with the Aboriginal Nancy and her children, he realised there had been a natural affinity. 'It was a common feeling and a satisfying feeling to know that we were with people we understood. We felt comfortable in that environment. We felt at ease with them.'

Then there was the reaction of others to the Palmers' somewhat swarthy complexion. 'People thought that we probably had European blood because Dad was dark and had a nose. He looked more Greek than he did Aboriginal. In discussions people would say, "Where are you from? What's your heritage?" and I'd say, "English and Scottish and a little bit of Swedish, I think, but mainly English."

'Anyway, you can see it now when you know what to look for. You look at any of my brothers and think he obviously has Aboriginal blood in him, except for Kirk, the youngest son. He's red-haired, freckled and looks very much like me.

'At first, I was in shock. Then I was dismayed. I thought, "I don't know how to believe this. What's this all about? Why now? What's the purpose of this?" I didn't understand what the rationale was, what the significance [was] of getting the family together now and telling us now when it should have been, in my view, right from the beginning.

'I feel proud of it now because there's nothing I can do to change anything. I mean, I'm proud of me as a person, as an individual, but the fact that there's Aboriginal heritage there doesn't make me more proud. I'm not ashamed to say that I have Aboriginal blood in my veins as I think my father was. And I think one of the main reasons he left it so long is because he couldn't bring it upon himself to tell us any earlier.

'Actually, I have since found out from him that he was very much embarrassed by the fact that he had Aboriginal blood, as a kid, because he lived in a tin shed on the edge of town and everybody would throw stones at him and, you know, ostracised him and he thought, "Bugger this. I'm not a blackfellow. I'm going to be a white man."'

Clint's attitudes to the Aboriginal people – and to the designation of Aboriginality – are ambivalent and controversial. 'We know in Australia, anybody of Aboriginal heritage can be known as Aboriginals. And I disagree with that because I think if you've got more than 50 per cent non-Aboriginal blood in your veins then you're a white man.'

He is critical of successive governments providing 'hand-outs' to the Aboriginal population. 'It's not the Aborigines' fault; it's because of the way the Australian Government has handled it over many years, and I think that now to give out handouts and royalties and all these benefits is bad behaviour on behalf of the Australian Government. Just to say, "Oh, sorry, mate. Look, here, take all this stuff and have a good life", that's rubbish. It's the wrong way to do it.

'You've got to take these people on board. Don't throw money at them. It doesn't solve anything!

'I think it's important for Aboriginal heritage to be recognised, but not for the purpose of remuneration – but rather so you know who you are! It has to be done properly because otherwise Aboriginal culture, as a separate culture, dies out. But in multicultural Australia, the future of this country is for everybody to live happily ever after in one big community. Now, if there's going to be cross-pollination, which inevitably has happened since mankind began, then eventually I guess that that minority race may dwindle away.'

When he broke the news to his family, their reaction was mixed. Callan didn't want to know, he says. Kelsee took it in her stride; Kimalee was shocked at first, 'But she came to terms with it quickly enough and [it] didn't seem to bother her,' Palmer says, 'except when she wanted to take the piss or got mad at me. Funny, really.'

•

The New Guinea posting was a long-standing SAS deployment. Despite being sidelined from the main thrust of
regimental activity in Iraq, he relished the appointment. 'In
terms of my career, it was the most satisfying,' he says. 'It
wasn't an upward step but it was all around good. It was an
overseas posting, and not everybody gets that, so I was quite
happy with that. I had the autonomy that I'd always wanted
in a job. I never have liked the feeling of people looking over
your shoulder and checking on you every two seconds along
the way. It really annoys me because when I say something
like, "I'll meet you there at 5 o'clock and I'll bring the beers
with me," I don't need the check. I'll be there are 5 o'clock
with the beers. If there's a problem, I'll ring or contact them
in some way. That's how I operate. I like to think that people
would treat me the way that I treat them.'

He would work from the massive Australian High
Commission in Port Moresby, one of the biggest of Australia's
overseas missions. He would set his own pace and maintain
clear reporting lines back to Swanbourne. His principal
task was to run Warrior Wing, a training cell set up by the
Australian Defence staff in New Guinea to support the
PNGDF in training up their reconnaisance elements.

'I would ensure the appropriate level of training and
courses to qualify PNG Defence Force personnel in the

arts of reconn,' he says. 'It was long-range patrolling; it was movement with stealth; it was survivability in the jungle; it was being able to locate and report back the locations of target areas whatever they might be,' he says. 'They lacked a little discipline every now and then, because they tend to lose concentration, and some aspects were quite demanding, but that was their way of life – We've had enough of this; let's clear off, sunbake, chase the wallabies through the bush – but that comes with the territory. It was basic stuff, but PNGDF guys just loved it; they sucked it up.'

They were not alone in that. 'I really enjoyed it,' he says, 'because I could plan ahead. I knew exactly where I was going. I could fit things in where I saw they were needed. It was awesome.'

Much of his time was spent in the field, where he would oversee PNG instructors running the courses. 'It was very flexible,' he says. 'Some days I'd be out in the bush on exercises. I might go away to Wee Wak for up to four weeks' running a recon course. Other times I'd be in my office where I had PNGDF instructors working with me, and I would do all the purchasing and administration, and they would actually do the instructional work. I'd help out but they would do all the instruction and run the course. I would oversee the men.'

There was another less obvious role in the job description. He was the regiment's 'eyes on' in one of Australia's most strategically sensitive locations. 'It's a volatile area, and at the time it was an unstable regime,' he says. 'And that's obviously one of the reasons they established the position up there.' By chance he was uniquely fitted for this 'undercover' aspect. 'I had an interest in Pidgin from way back when Dad told us stories of his father in New Guinea during the war,' he says. 'A guy I worked with at Canungra in 1981 gave me a copy of a PNG newspaper written in Tok Pisin (Pidgin), and I learned from reading that over and over. I did a five-day colloquial course just prior to the 1986 trip when we climbed the mountain, but for the most part I was self-taught.'

This allowed him to communicate beneath the 'expat' surface and the reportage added spice to the mix. What followed was 'a great two years'. The one professional frustration was that he could not extend his training courses to parachuting; the terrain and the changeable weather conditions meant that parachuting was off limits. The PNG Defence Force had no mandate for that aspect of combat training. There were also some good times in his private life. They had spacious, comfortable quarters with plenty of help in the house. Security was not a problem for an SAS operative. And for the first time in some years he was able to enjoy a settled family life. 'We had a lot of time together,' he says. 'We went away on holidays together at that stage; Callan and Kelsee enjoyed the experience of a new country and a different culture.' Kimalee even joined him on an expedition on the Kokoda Track, with diplomatic and Defence personnel from the High Commission.

When his two years were up he applied for an extension of a further year. The request was denied, but the sojourn away from the cut and thrust of the regiment had given him the chance to recover from the Afghanistan imbroglio, to take stock of his career and to look ahead. 'My goal was to become a warrant officer class 1 and a regimental sergeant major,' he says. 'If I got that far then I'd try to secure the RSM position at Swanbourne.'

He canvassed the possibility with his superiors. 'I put my hand up and gave my justification and a plan and it was rejected,' he says. 'They didn't offer me that position and, of course, to be RSM there, you're supposed to have been CSM – an SSM of the squadron – which I wasn't. There are exceptions – one guy did make it without ever being an SSM of a Sabre squadron, but he was the last of the Vietnam vets and he got the job.' They were not about to make a similar exception for Clint Palmer. However, the job they did offer him really played to his strength: RSM of the Parachute Training School in Nowra. It meant a promotion to WO1 and a highly responsible task in an area that he enjoyed.

It wasn't all good. He would be away from the centre of the action at Swanbourne at a time when the regiment's role in Iraq was reaching a peak, and Afghanistan was coming back into focus as the Taliban and al-Qaeda reasserted themselves in the countryside. But the posting was only for two years, and there was always the chance that he would then return to a combat zone. However, the real hammer blow came from within. Kimalee was determined to take the kids and return to Perth, and did not accompany him to Nowra.

17

TROUBLED LANDS

While WO Clint Palmer was wrestling with this latest bump in a rocky road, the regiment itself was preoccupied with navigating its way through the war in Iraq, while at the same time taking note of the increasing Taliban insurgency in Afghanistan. Clearly, they would need to prepare for a second deployment to that troubled land where armed conflict – against invaders or rival clans – had been a way of life for millennia. But for the moment the focus was on Iraq, where the SASR would provide the majority of the ground force element of the government's response.

Once again the CO, Lieutenant Colonel Gus Gilmore, and his operations officer Major Tinley had acted as pathfinders for the mission with a trip to the Americans' military headquarters. The regiment's record in Afghanistan gave them immediate entrée to the planning team at Operation Iraqi Liberation (soon renamed Operation Iraqi Freedom) in Florida. They were welcomed and incorporated into the reconstituted Task Force Dagger, the driving force behind Anaconda, which, in the Orwellian world of the military, had now been elevated from fiasco to glittering triumph. Dagger had special responsibility for Western Iraq and while much of its operation remains classified, the SAS dominated the Australian Special Forces Task Group, which included a support troop from the Incident Response Regiment and a platoon from the 4th Battalion RAR.

Once the commitment was secured, Gus Gilmore moved on to Special Forces command in Canberra; Lieutenant Colonel Rick Burr took over as CO; and on 18 March 2003 Prime Minister Howard, despite previous denials, finally announced publicly that Australia had joined the 'Coalition of the Willing' and would commit troops to the Iraqi invasion. In fact, 1 Squadron had already entered Iraq from Jordan when the Prime Minister made his announcement.

By now former CO Mike Hindmarsh had been promoted to Brigadier, and was at Coalition headquarters in Qatar, where he was able to monitor the progress of the SAS patrols as they crossed the desert and engaged enemy facilities. 'I was bloody concerned,' he says. 'We all were . . . These guys were going into harm's way. [The Iraqis] would have learned from the previous Gulf War what we were likely to be doing, and the intelligence reports we were getting indicated that that was the case.'[34]

In the event, they carried out their mission without loss and secured the massive Al Asad air base with powerful American air support and very little resistance on the ground. There were a couple of near-miss 'friendly fire' incidents, but fortunately no one was hurt. They established roadblocks to prevent Saddam Hussein's confederates fleeing from Baghdad where the American 'Shock and Awe' bombing raids devastated the city and disrupted his command and control centres.

As in Afghanistan, US Special Forces – together with SF units from Britain and other Coalition nations – played a major role in the provincial areas. The Australians again distinguished themselves, and on 9 April Baghdad fell to the Allies. US forces seized the deserted Ba'ath Party ministries and stage-managed the tearing down of a huge iron statue of Saddam Hussein, who had gone into hiding.

On 1 May President Bush staged a melodramatic event on the aircraft carrier USS *Abraham Lincoln* and declared – somewhat prematurely – 'Mission accomplished'. With the commander-in-chief having decided the war was at an end, the majority of the SAS team returned from Iraq and were not replaced. However, it is believed that a small group remained to provide intelligence on the aftermath of the

American battlefield victory as well as counter-insurgency and training operations.

On their return to Australia 1 Squadron led a parade at Swanbourne to celebrate the award of a Unit Citation for Gallantry presented by Governor-General Peter Hollingworth. It was one of Hollingworth's final acts before handing over the role of Australia's titular commander-in-chief to the former SAS recruit Michael Jeffrey. He was sworn in on 11 August 2003.

Back in Iraq, Australia confined its post-invasion deployment to a single C-130 Hercules transport flying humanitarian supplies into Baghdad and specialists attached to the Coalition headquarters helping in the vain search for the Weapons of Mass Destruction. However, Prime Minister Howard gradually increased the commitment, including a frigate in the Persian Gulf, a party of air traffic controllers at Baghdad International Airport, two AP-3C Orion aircraft and a small security detachment of infantry and airfield defence guards protecting the Australian diplomats in Baghdad. Then came an army training unit and a small medical team attached to a US Air Force hospital.

On 13 December 2003, Saddam Hussein was captured by American forces in a hole in the ground at a farmhouse in his home town of Tikrit. He was taken into custody at an American base near Baghdad and questioned for six months before being handed over to the interim Iraqi Government to stand trial for crimes against humanity. Charges included the murder of 148 people, the torture of women and children, and the illegal arrest of 399 others. His interrogators found no evidence whatever of his involvement with al-Qaeda or the attack on New York's twin towers. He would be tried by an Iraqi court in 2006, found guilty and hanged on 30 December.

In 2004, the most serious fighting of the war began when in March insurgents in Fallujah ambushed a convoy led by four private military contractors. All four were killed and their burned corpses hung from a bridge over the Euphrates River. In November the Americans launched the bloodiest battle of the war to date – 46 days of close combat warfare in Fallujah that took the lives of 95 Americans and more than 1,000 Iraqi insurgents.

It followed the revelations of widespread prisoner abuse at Abu Ghraib, a major blow to the Americans, who now pressured the Australian Government to increase its commitment. In February 2005, Howard announced the deployment of a 500-strong battle group to the relatively peaceful Al Muthanna Province to provide security for the Japanese engineers working there. As well, they would help train local Iraqi security forces. They began operations two months later, but following the withdrawal of the Japanese force and the transfer of Al Muthanna to Iraqi control they relocated to

Tallil Air Base in neighbouring Dhi Qar Province in July 2006 as the Overwatch Battle Group (West).

As the intensity and pace of insurgent attacks increased, the war was veering out of control. Similarly in Afghanistan, the insurgency gradually increased as the Taliban resuscitated its network through the towns and villages from its strongholds in the border provinces of Pakistan. The rallying cry was for a jihad (holy war), against the puppet Afghan Government and the infidels who pulled its strings. Training camps of up to 200 recruits and instructors were established in the mountains of the east to accommodate the volunteers streaming into them from the madrassas of Pakistan's tribal region.

By late 2004, Taliban fighters had built up their forces in Zabul Province and spread their attacks to neighbouring Oruzgan, the traditional heartland of the cult. More than 200 casualties among Afghan police and government loyalists were recorded in a single month. The Bush administration, preoccupied with Iraq, was slow to respond, but in mid-2005 Afghan Government forces backed by US troops and heavy aerial bombardment advanced on Taliban positions in the mountains.

Australia also returned to the fray. On 13 July Prime Minister John Howard announced that a 190-member Special Forces element would return to Afghanistan for 12 months in support of the 'legitimate government in Afghanistan

[that] has come under increasing attack and pressure from the Taliban in particular and some elements of al-Qaeda'.

In late August 2005, Afghan Government forces backed by US troops and heavy American aerial bombardment advanced upon Taliban positions within the mountain fortresses. After a one-week battle, Taliban forces were routed, with up to 124 fighters killed (according to Afghan Government estimates).

In September, the SASR redeployed there as part of the Australian Special Operations Task Group (SOTG) which also included the 4th Battalion RAR – later to gain regimental status as 2nd Commando – the Incident Response Regiment and logistic support personnel. 2 Squadron was the active SAS ingredient in the task force and they arrived via Qatar, where there was now a large contingent of administration staff and RAAF personnel. During the stopover they were attached to the huge American camp, so big that it supported several separate messes. From there they boarded C-130s for the final stage of the journey to Tarin Kot in Oruzgan Province, where the Australians would make their principal contribution to the war.

Within a few days they were out on patrol in their LRPVs, passing old T55 Russian tanks rusting at the side of the roads or half buried at river crossings. The country was a mix of extremes: stark, bare, rocky mountains rising to enormous heights above valleys – 'the green' – bursting with lush vegetation at each side of a rushing stream. Usually the women stayed inside the compounds, but nothing had changed since Clint had noted the kids who stared at the foreigners as they roared by while the men – bearded and surly – either ignored them or deliberately turned their backs.

On occasion the patrols operated in concert with members of the Afghan National Army and in some of the bigger missions with a combination of 4RAR and American JTACs (joint terminal attack controllers) to call in air support as needed. Contacts with Taliban fighters were spasmodic and rarely fatal to the Coalition. The most hazardous weapon was the IED, which would take more Allied lives than any other in the insurgents' armoury.

On the other side of the world, Clint Palmer had 'intensive discussions' with wife Kimalee over her decision in Papua New Guinea to return to Perth with the children. It was bad enough to be sidelined in Nowra, but to have the family 4,000 kilometres away was hard to take.

'The kids would have loved it,' he says. 'It's got Jervis Bay nearby, a lovely part of the world, a coastline north to Gerringong and south to Bateman's Bay and that beautiful hinterland.'

Even his promotion to WO1 was a double-edged sword. While he had achieved a long-standing ambition, the higher rank meant there were fewer positions available in the SASR, so a return to Swanbourne was going to be more difficult to secure. Well, he would face that when the time came. For the moment the demands of the job kept him fully occupied. And, after all, he consoled himself, it was a discipline that he not only relished but had been at the core of the SAS since its founding in 1942.

As RSM he was not directly concerned with parachute training. 'The school is run administratively by the headquarters and the Training Wing sits under the headquarters,' he says. 'The CO runs the show; the RSM is the man in charge of discipline and soldier management in the unit.' However, his intense interest in all aspects of parachuting meant he was able to provide a guiding hand where necessary.

'I had the position in the regiment there of subject matter expert,' he says. 'It's called "Subject Master Air Operations". I did that job any number of times, and to that extent I was probably seen to be the senior, current guy in parachuting in the unit at the time; and the responsibilities of that particular job meant I had to conduct the parachute training for the regiment. I was recognised as the senior and most qualified and experienced guy in parachuting in the unit – not always, but normally.'

The vital first priority was packing the parachute. 'It's customary in the skydiving world for each jumper to pack his own parachute,' he says. 'As a civilian this skill is normally taught in the initial phase of training, and the individual packs every parachute that he jumps. In the military, however, there are qualified parachute riggers whose job it is to pack parachutes, maintain the parachutes in good working order and repair any damage to parachutes which may be reusable.

'There are many steps in packing a parachute and as a safety measure there are many checks conducted after each major step. This quality control ensures that the probability of an incident is reduced as much as possible. It takes a lot of practice and repetition to learn the sequence. The most important rule is to respect the parachute and handle it with care.

'The procedures are laid down in a logical sequence, the same as taking the wheel off a car then putting it back on. After each jump the parachute is laid out and the lines are checked to ensure there are no tangles or knots, and that the parachute is free from damage. After the line check the brakes are set. They are normally found at the rear of the parachute and are used to steer left and right as well as apply the force to stop the parachute from flying. The canopy is then folded in accordance with the manufacturer's specifications to ensure a clean opening sequence.

'Once the canopy is folded, it is then packed into a deployment bag and the lines are stowed in an S-fold to prevent tangles during the opening. The deployment bag and the lines are packed into the parachute container and the container closed. The final check is done and the parachute logbook is then signed off. This is done to maintain a current and historical record of the number of jumps the parachute has done and who has packed it for each jump. Each one of these stages is checked by a rigger supervisor – never the person who is packing.'

Recently the regiment introduced a 'user repack' qualification. 'Those guys who are advanced, qualified and have a significant number of jumps up can learn to pack their parachutes,' he says. 'But it has to be done with the supervision of a qualified parachute rigger because there are steps in the sequence of packing a parachute that need to be checked.'

Once he had established a routine, Clint travelled to Perth several times to be with the family. 'At times it felt like we were going through the motions and didn't have a long-term goal,' he says. 'The water looked pretty muddy. On the surface it probably seemed like the normal husband and wife with a couple of kids coping with all the challenges life throws at you.'

The reality was very different. 'In the end,' he says, 'it was my decision to leave – on 12 January 2006.'

18

FLARE-UP ABROAD

After their formal separation, Palmer returned to Nowra to serve out the remainder of his two-year posting. It was a tough 11 months. He lived in a room on HMAS *Albatross*, the Naval Air Station, which operated as the base for the Parachute Training School. He buried himself in his work. He spent his spare time in his quarters or the mess and fretted about Callan and daughter Kelsee. He was entitled to six brief trips 'home' a year, so travelled back to Perth every six to eight weeks, staying with his father. Kimalee and the children remained in the family home.

'I missed the whole family and in particular the kids, because I knew that they didn't really understand the reasons for what had happened So every time I came home I had time with them', he says.

In August Kimalee decided to move from the army quarters.

Back in Nowra, 'The time dragged,' he says. 'I really couldn't wait to get a posting back to Perth to be near the kids.' That's when the full force of his circumstances hit home. The promotion to WO1 meant he had reached the top of a pyramid, as high as a non-commissioned officer could go; and at his age there was no chance (even if he wanted it) that he would be a candidate for a commission. But the jobs available for someone at his rank were few and far between. And in the regiment they were all filled.

'The only [SAS] option for me was to take a position in headquarters Special Operations Command in Sydney', he says. 'So from Nowra, I go to Sydney; I'd still be away from my family.' In Perth there was only one possibility: 13 Brigade, a reserve formation with its headquarters in suburban Karrakatta. 'I really didn't have any choice,' he says, 'so I took it.'

13 Brigade had a proud history. Created in 1916 after the evacuation of Gallipoli, by May that year it was fighting in a sector of the French Western Front at Petillon; and it played a vital role in retaking Villers-Bretonneux during the second battle of the Somme. At the end of the war it was disbanded, but reformed in 1939 at the outbreak of the hostilities in Europe. Until 1942, when Broome was bombed, it was the

only army unit in place to protect the Western Australian coastline from the feared Japanese invasion.

The current brigade was formed in 1988 as part of the Australian Army's 2nd Division and is tasked with the protection of Western Australia. It administers all the state's reserve units with depots in Geraldton, Kalgoorlie, Albany and Katanning as well as Joondalup and Rockingham in the metropolitan area. However, for a soldier of Clint's training and experience it was a military purgatory.

'I lasted only three or four days there,' he says. That's when he used his contacts in the SASR to manipulate the military red tape to mutual advantage. 'I rang up the regiment and spoke to the RSM. I said, "Bill, I've got to get out of here."'

The RSM was happy to have him and soon found a place for him in the Operations Support Squadron. 'So while I was posted to 13 Brigade I was actually working in Swanbourne,' Clint says. 'I was running a little parachuting as well as demolitions courses – a bit of this, a bit of that, anything they wanted me to do.' The arrangement lasted throughout 2007, and in January the following year he returned officially to the SAS as the training cell warrant officer at regimental headquarters.

It was a key position. It required him to coordinate all the major assets needed throughout a training calendar year – from helicopters for air mobile training, C-130s for parachuting operations, submarines and other vessels for water-based exercises. 'It was the coordination of all that,' he says, 'bearing in mind all the lead times through the booking process; then following through and changing things to make sure everything the guys asked for we'd get for them at the appropriate time.'

He was good at his job and threw himself into it. He did whatever it took to mobilise the military bureaucracy, from personal contacts to a judicious mix of persuasion, good fellowship and, if necessary, sharp command. It was testing work but he enjoyed it. He had served his time in the regiment's outer darkness; now he was back in the mainstream, if not the purple circle exactly then certainly a place of respect from the regimental hierarchy. They in turn had been working at full stretch, their focus principally on the continuing conflicts in Iraq and Afghanistan, but also on a sudden flare-up in East Timor.

In February 2006, 404 Timorese Government soldiers from the regular strength of about 1,500 had deserted their barracks, and by the end of the month had been joined by a further 177. Civil war threatened, and in April fighting broke out between the rebels and government soldiers. On 4 May the rebels were strengthened by the defection of Major Alfredo Reinado, together with 20 military police, who brought with them two trucks full of weapons and ammunition.

Reinado set up a headquarters in the town of Aileu in the mountainous area south of Dili, while armed gangs terrorised the capital. And, as the situation deteriorated still further, Foreign Minister Ramos Horta sought assistance from Australia, New Zealand, Malaysia and Portugal. The SAS deployed direct to Dili from HMAS *Manoora*, and on the afternoon of 25 May, four Black Hawk helicopters and a C-130 Hercules landed at Dili airport with the first wave of Australian forces. They were attacked as they endeavoured to keep the gangs separated while they helped civilians escape to safety through back alleys. The Australians did not return fire, instead discouraging the gangs by advancing towards them and shouting orders and threats. The rescued civilians were then rushed to the nearby UN compound.

On 29 May the Australian CO, Brigadier Michael Slater, met with civilian and military leaders in Dili and negotiated a return to barracks by the rebels. The political unrest continued, and on 22 June President Gusmão announced on television that he would resign the following day unless Alkatiri vacated his prime ministerial post. This brought the crisis to a head and placed irresistible pressure on Alkatiri, who stepped down four days later. Peace gradually returned; Reinardo surrendered and the SAS contingent withdrew early in July.

In the Middle East, the Iraqi war had been going badly. While Prime Minister Howard had largely insulated the Australians from casualties by insisting on a relatively peaceful area of operations for the task force, the Americans and British allies were suffering serious loss of life and the inevitable political backlash.

On 23 January 2007 in his State of the Union address to Congress, President George W. Bush announced a 'surge' of more than 20,000 additional American soldiers and marines to combat the insurgency.

In Britain, the Labour Government of Prime Minister Tony Blair, one of the most enthusiastic proponents of the initial invasion, bowed to pressure within his party and announced his troops would soon begin to withdraw from their principal area of operations in the southern Basra region. By now the Danish Government had withdrawn its 440 troops, leaving only a nine-man helicopter unit. Other allies were also voicing the intention to depart

The rate of US combat deaths in Baghdad nearly doubled in the first seven weeks of the surge, although across the rest of Iraq it remained relatively stable. Then on 14 August the deadliest single attack of the whole war occurred. Nearly 800 civilians were killed by a series of coordinated suicide bomb attacks on the northern Iraqi settlement of Kahtaniya. More than 100 homes and shops were destroyed in the blasts. US officials blamed al-Qaeda. Others suggested it was the result of a sectarian feud when members of the Yazidi community stoned to death a teenage girl over her relations with a Sunni Arab. Either way, it was a blow to the American cause.

The Australian forces in Iraq took full responsibility for security in Dhi Qar Province when the Italian forces withdrew in July 2006. Dhi Qar adjoined Al Muthana, where they had been entrenched since the beginning of the deployment and which had remained relatively peaceful. By late 2006 the Australian mission, codenamed Operation Catalyst, had risen to 1,400. However, moves to hand both provinces over to Iraqi security forces were well advanced by mid-2007. And during the federal election that year Opposition Leader Kevin Rudd campaigned on a policy of withdrawing all Australian troops from the Iraqi conflict.

Rudd was successful and, as prime minister, began to withdraw combat forces from Iraq on 1 June 2008. The Overwatch Battle Group (West) and Australian Army Training Team formally ceased combat operations on 2 June 2008, having helped train 33,000 Iraqi soldiers. Some 200 Australian personnel remained in Iraq on logistical and air surveillance duties.

By contrast, Rudd committed the Australian Labor Party to unequivocal support for the war in Afghanistan, which by this time was entering a new phase of ever increasing violence from Taliban and al-Qaeda forces. In April 2006 Australia had deployed a Special Operations Task Group with the SAS at the core. Operating from Tarin Kot in Oruzgan Province, they were now in the firing line against an enemy that exploited all the advantages of a guerrilla force operating on its own soil.

During that summer, Coalition forces scored some notable victories with the elimination of top-level Taliban commanders, and in the Battle of Chora in Oruzgan Province, where Australian and Dutch forces combined with some Afghan National Army units to engage the biggest Taliban battle group of 2006. Fought over five days and nights from 15 June, it cost the lives of 20 Allied soldiers, 58 civilians and an unknown number of Taliban fighters. One Australian was killed and six wounded. However, it preserved land access to Tarin Kot and allowed Australian SAS patrols to press deeper into the province.

In January and February 2007, the Allies began a series of operations on Taliban strongholds across the country aimed at blunting the expected spring offensive from the insurgents. In March, the Bush administration sent an additional 3,500 troops into the war zone, and the British raised their commitment to 7,700.

By then the Taliban were estimated to have about 10,000 fighters in the field, about 3,000 of whom were full-time soldiers, the rest part-timers, made up of young Afghan men alienated by bombing raids, the presence of foreign troops or the death of relatives, or simply fighting for money. But throughout 2007, an increasing number of fighters from other Muslim nations were arriving in Afghanistan to support the insurgents. By year's end at least 300 full-time combatants had come from Pakistan, Uzbekistan, Chechnya, various Arab countries and possibly even Turkey and western China. According to intelligence sources, they were more fanatical and violent than the Afghans and brought sophisticated skills to the conflict, from video propaganda on the Internet to advanced bomb-making expertise.

The focus of the international war on terror was now clearly moving from Iraq to Afghanistan. In the first five months of 2008, the Americans increased their deployment by almost 80 per cent to a massive 48,250 in June. In September 2008, President Bush announced the withdrawal of over 8,000 troops from Iraq in the coming months and a further increase of up to 4,500 US troops in Afghanistan. In June 2008, British Prime Minister Gordon Brown announced an increase of British troops in Afghanistan to just over 8,000.

On 13 June, Taliban fighters demonstrated their strength, particularly in the south, by liberating all prisoners in the Kandahar jail. The well-planned operation freed 1,200 prisoners, 400 of whom were Taliban POWs, causing a major embarrassment for NATO in one of its operational centres.

Australian SAS patrols were confronting the enemy in Oruzgan Province and disrupting their fighting season plans. However, the operations came at a cost. On 25 October 2007 Sergeant Matt Locke was fatally wounded by rifle fire in a contact with Taliban during Operation Spin Ghar, designed to clear the Taliban from around Tarin Kot.

On 8 July 2008, SAS Signaller Sean McCarthy was killed when an IED exploded beneath his LRPV. The driver and the vehicle commander were thrown from the car and injured. The Afghan interpreter in the rear seat lost the lower part of both of his legs.

Two months later, nine SAS soldiers were wounded, three seriously, during a major ambush of their patrol by insurgents in what became known as the Battle of Khaz Uruzgan. The patrols were part of a combined American and ANA operation out of FOB Anaconda designed to 'flush out' Taliban fighters. In the first element of the mission, Australian snipers accounted for 11 enemy soldiers. However, when the Allied forces were making their way back to base through the Khaz Oruzgan valley they were surrounded on three sides by between 150 and 200 fighters.

With only one way to go the patrol turned all guns towards the enemy fire. However, they were pinned down by blistering small arms fire, RPGs and mortars. Eventually, an American JTAC called in two F/A-18 Hornets, and they made two 20-millimetre cannon runs into Taliban positions. He followed this with a 500-pound airburst bomb on a mortar position.

By this stage they were 90 minutes into the battle and the SAS patrols were taking the brunt of the enemy fire.

Training with Filipino special forces in 2001.

Clint Palmer as a patrol commander *(second from right)* in the Kimberley region, Western Australia.

On board the USS *Missouri* in 1986.

Airborne rappelling, Goldie River, Papua New Guinea, in 1986.

Clint Palmer was not always well behaved . . .
result of an adventurous night out!

An outstanding achievement – climbing Mt Victoria in
Papua New Guinea in 1986.

Early family photo (*left to right*): Isabel, Blake, Garry, Nita (*front*), Clint, Kirk, Terry and Dean.

A young Clint Palmer with dad, Terry, at Burleigh Heads on the Gold Coast.

The proud soldier with mother, Isabel, and sister Brenda, in August 1984.

Clint Palmer with his former wife, Kimalee,
at the SAS Regimental Ball in 1987.

Three generations on Christmas Day, Perth 2012 – Clint Palmer and his father, son Callan and daughter Kelsee.

Just seconds away from possible death – two parachutists collide, Christchurch, New Zealand in 1996. Clint Palmer is on top, trying to free himself.

A twenty-way formation over Jervis Bay, celebrating Parachute Training School's twenty years at Naval Air Station, Nowra.

Skydiving in the French countryside, La Ferté-Gaucher, 1993.
Clint Palmer is on the left.

Clint with daughter Kelsee at York, Western Australia – just before boarding for her first jump on 20 November 2012.

Clint and Callan on the day of his first jump.

They noticed a pair of Dutch Apache helicopters at 15,000 feet and signalled for them to give assistance. However, the pilots claimed they were required to stay at altitude, and the full-throated exchange between the Australians and the pilots would later cause an embarrassing diplomatic interchange.[35]

Finally the vehicles lined up and made a dash for the valley floor and across the bare terrain to the FOB. Nine of the 13 Australians in the battle had been wounded and three were evacuated to hospitals in Kandahar and Germany.

During the contact one Afghan interpreter had been thrown out the back of an Australian vehicle and, despite overwhelming enemy fire, SAS Trooper Mark Donaldson ran more than 100 metres back to rescue him and carry him to safety. Donaldson was later awarded the Victoria Cross for Australia.

In November 2008, WO Clint Palmer received his new assignment. Six years and six months after his controversial departure from Afghanistan in the wake of Operation Anaconda, he was on his way back.

19

RETURN TO THE MIDDLE EAST

Palmer's reassignment was ordered by the Regiment's new CO, Lieutenant Colonel Paul Burns, universally regarded as 'a great bloke – smart and very personable'. According to Clint, 'in some respects he was way ahead of his time. I think some guys at the unit saw him as a visionary and not in touch with reality.'

This is understandable. Unlike some of his predecessors, Burns was a highly accomplished academic and thought deeply about the optimal use of Special Forces in their continuing struggle against a more flexible and adaptable enemy such as al-Qaeda. This is best illustrated in a 2007 paper (later posted on the internet) that he wrote as part of his Master of Operation Studies at the US Marine Corps' School of Advanced War fighting at Quantico, Virginia.[36]

In this 'Future War' thesis, he criticised current Special Forces training and operations as being too rigid and becoming less 'special'. '[They] could arguably be more appropriately characterised as "conventional elite",' he wrote. 'Special operations are being continually superseded by a military evolutionary process that requires once uniquely special skills, approaches and equipment to be handed off as conventional forces adopt them.'

He advocated the development of a new approach termed Complex Adaptive Special Operations (CASO) in which SF units would be 'near-autonomous', with little direction from the military chain of command. They would comprise teams of specially selected personnel, each possessing unique military and non-military expertise, who would operate 'like a virus within an ecosystem', under 'general guidelines' that would permit them to determine their own behaviour in actions against the enemy. In many respects they would become the mirror image of their adversary.

To what degree (if any) his proposals were accepted by Australia's defence establishment is unknown. At a time when warfare is increasingly conducted under technology's watchful eye and political transparency is an article of faith, it is unlikely that its special forces would be given such a free hand. But the SAS values both initiative and secrecy in equal measure and Burns's proposals are no more than a logical extension of the Regiment's ethos and *modus operandi*.

Certainly in Afghanistan under Burn's watch SAS patrols were called upon to operate at the limits of their brief. And it is a measure of their professionalism and dedication that there were never any suggestions that they exceeded their rules of engagement. Indeed, Paul Burns, who later left the Regiment for private enterprise, remains a highly regarded figure in the evolution of the SASR.

His assignment of Palmer as deputy to the Special Operations Liaison Officer (SOLO) covered both Operation Catalyst in Iraq, where more than 200 Australian personnel remained after the departure of the frontline troops, and Operation Slipper in Afghanistan, which was at the peak of activity. He would divide his time between the two for the next six months.

'I was posted to the Australian headquarters in the Middle East, Joint Task Force (JTF) 633 which was located in Baghdad,' he says, 'but my responsibility was to go between the two theatres to do my job so I spent a fair amount of time in both places.'

The Australian HQ in Iraq was in the grounds of one of Saddam Hussein's former palaces known as Al Faw in Camp Victory. 'It was a 20 k mad dash down route Irish from the Green Zone,' he says. 'It was co-located with the American Corps headquarters, which were in the palace itself. We were located in one of the smaller palace buildings on the lake, adjacent to the main headquarters where Saddam kept the harem.' He laughs. 'Actually, there was a hotel right next door where they kept the girlies. They'd come in from time to time, not live there, but in Saddam Hussein's real house at the time, he had it all set up.'

The palace buildings themselves were an eye-opener. 'They spent a lot of time and effort building these things and they were all nice, all marble facades, but there was concrete reinforcement,' he says. 'Actually they were concrete structures with marble plates on the outside so it looked nice, carved in relief, very typically Middle Eastern, opulent in some ways but a little bit different from how we lived. They had large rooms with plenty of space.

'We lived and worked there. We had an accommodation block adjacent to it, called Australia House. And there was another smaller palace guest house arrangement. It was cylindrical and it was known as The Round House. A few people lived in there. But all the Australians who worked in the headquarters – between 30 and 40 – lived in this area. It was quite good. There was a swimming pool there, it was a good set-up.'

The Australian contingent comprised the commander, his operational command team, clerical support and transport organisers, caterers and logistics personnel of both sexes. In addition, senior officers were embedded with the American and Coalition commands but also lived in Australia House.

'The Iraqis had their own headquarters in the same compound,' he says, 'and of course there was constant liaising with them because we were in their country and the whole deal was to get them back stably on their feet and order restored.'

However, with the Iraqi commitment coming to an end, the Australian HQ was on the move. The control centre for all Middle East operations was being transferred to Al Minhad, a massive air base in the United Arab Emirates 25 kilometres south of Dubai. There conditions were very different. 'We were mostly in demountables, two to a room while construction was going on,' Palmer says. The new HQ would eventually become a well-structured 500-person base with a mess, a gym and other facilities. But in the early days it was 'fairly primitive'. And while he used it as a base, his liaison work meant that he was travelling constantly.

His SAS status gave him special responsibilities including contingency plans for emergency evacuation of Australians out of the region, as well as other liaison tasks with the coalition. 'The job was demanding and important, too', he says, 'as it was in direct support of all Australians in the MEAO, not just our guys in SOTG.'

During his third visit to the American HQ in Baghdad, he noticed a familiar figure. 'I saw him from behind in the great marble foyer there,' Palmer says. 'I said, "G'day, Frank" and he turned around and recognised me immediately.' It was Frank Grippe, the American RSM with whom he'd shared Hell's Halfpipe in the Battle of Anaconda. By now he was the RSM to the entire American operation in Iraq and he had a retinue around him. 'He said, "Goddamn!" and gave me this bear hug,' he recalls. 'Then it's, "Hey, everyone, come and meet my Aussie mate Clint. He's a goddamn hero. He saved our asses in Anaconda. Goddamn, it's great to see you, buddy."'

Suddenly all the anguish he had endured in those six intervening years was swept away as the American regaled his listeners with the story of that desperate battle and his part in it. And later they went to Frank's vast office overlooking Baghdad, where he opened a bottle of the finest pure water and box of Havana cigars. 'By now LaCamara is gone,' Palmer says. 'He didn't have to worry about his loyalty to the individual. That was history. He'd done the right thing at the time. The American glue stuck fast. But he was quite candid with me about it.

'LaCamera, he said, didn't want his performance to be overshadowed by this Australian warrant officer who had a succinct understanding of the battlespace at that time and was able to offer solutions to problems then and there . . . just didn't want to know about it . . . would have made him look worthless, like some dumbo.' The Australian soaked it in as the watermark on the pure water bottle headed south. When he finally departed it was with a sense of confidence restored and self-esteem confirmed.

Thereafter he was constantly on the move. His normal transport was by C-130 transport and occasionally a smaller charter aircraft. 'I travelled to Kabul, to Bagram, Kandahar, everywhere there was a job to be done,' he says. 'Sometimes it was a bit tiring going through all the procedures in a war zone. It was demanding in the hours because you're expected to be available and be around. When things were happening, you had to be there all the time and sometimes – for instance, if an incident occurred in Afghanistan and they were reporting back to Headquarters 633 – the operation was 24/7.'

Moreover, if his boss was travelling he had to take over. 'If the SOLO was away I was the man,' he says. 'I had to be there for any issue that came up or options to be put to the commander. And if we had casualties – not just from the SAS or the Special Operations Task Group but any of the Australians in Afghanistan – then we were closely involved. So while my specific job was dealing directly with Special Forces, I had to plan for all contingencies. If the requirement was to extract Australian diplomats or politicians who might be travelling in the area, we were looking at all the options. If an incident occurred in a particular town, how would we mount an operation? We needed to know all the planning aspects surrounding it. It was a very interesting job and it kept you on your toes.'

Operating in a war zone – particularly Iraq – also brought personal dangers. 'There was always stuff going on in the background,' he says. 'You'd hear the explosions or whatever. Something might go off about 800 metres down the road but it never happened close to me, where I had to render assistance – you didn't get involved with things you didn't need to. But there was one time when I was flying into Baghdad; we were making our approach and there was a huge, metallic bang-thud back in the aircraft. I was just lying down, relaxing and jumped up and checked to see what was happening. The pilots up front were jabbering at 100 miles per hour and talking to the control tower for assistance. Next minute we turned around. We'd only been 15 minutes out of Baghdad but we flew all the way back to Kuwait, landed the aircraft in the middle of the quarantine zone and got everyone off really quick.

'I jumped on another aircraft and took off back to Baghdad. I found out later some sort of round from a large calibre weapon hit the back of the airplane.'

Palmer's deployment was coming to an end in June 2009. By now the Australian contingent had all moved from Iraq to Al Minhad in the UAE, where HQ JTF 633 was taking shape. They left behind a shattered country that was struggling to reshape its constituent parts into a workable entity. In February, the new US President Barack Obama had reaffirmed his determination to end the war, promising that the U.S. combat mission in Iraq would end by 31 August 2010. A 'transitional force' of up to 50,000 troops tasked with training the Iraqi Security Forces, conducting counterterrorism operations, and providing general support would remain until the end of 2011.

However, on 9 April, the sixth anniversary of Baghdad's fall, tens of thousands of Iraqis thronged the capital's streets and squares to burn effigies of George W. Bush and demand the immediate withdrawal of all Coalition forces. On 30 April Britain formally ended combat operations and handed control of Basra to the US, with the British Prime Minister Gordon Brown claiming that the intervention was a 'success story'.

On 28 July Australia withdrew its combat forces on schedule. By then US troops had also completed their withdrawal from Iraqi cities, passing responsibility for security to the government of Prime Minister Nouri al-Maliki, who declared 30 June National Sovereignty Day.

However, on 19 August two massive bomb attacks killed at least 95 and wounded more than 600 in Baghdad. The violence had been steadily escalating in previous weeks and worse was to come. In October two suicide bombings in the capital, orchestrated by al-Qaeda, killed more than 150 and injured at least 700. In December, five bombs in and around government buildings in Baghdad killed 120 people and cut down 400 more, with Sunni insurgents claiming responsibility.

Nevertheless, Iraqis were heading toward national elections and a semblance of a sustainable polity was beginning to take shape. By contrast, the situation in Afghanistan was becoming steadily more chaotic as the Taliban, with extremist Islamist assistance from abroad, attacked ISAF forces and spread their net through disaffected communities. They were assisted by a combination of tribalism, corruption within the Karzai Government and funding from the home-grown opium/heroin trade.

On 10 August 2009, General Stanley McChrystal, the newly appointed US commander in Afghanistan, said that the Taliban had gained the upper hand. 'In a continuation of the Taliban's usual strategy of summer offensives, the militants have aggressively spread their influence into the north and west of Afghanistan,' he said, 'and stepped up their attack in an attempt to disrupt the 20 August presidential polls.'

Calling the Taliban a 'very aggressive enemy', he said the US strategy in the months to come 'is to stop their momentum and focus on protecting and safeguarding Afghan civilians.'

As predicted, the Taliban claimed that it effectively disrupted the 20 August elections with more than 135 violent incidents. And independent observers reported that the elector turnout was well below the 70 per cent expected. Indeed, in the Taliban strongholds in the south it was well below 50 per cent. The chief observer of the European Union election mission, General Philippe Morillon, said the election was 'generally fair' but 'not free'.

However, while the Taliban might have had some success in delegitimising the poll, the principal contenders, Hamid Karzai and Abdullah Abdullah, indulged in such widespread fraud and standover tactics that the result was little more than a democratic farce. Both claimed victory but Karzai held the reins – and the purse strings – of government. Abdullah Abdullah went quietly.

By now Palmer had returned to Swanbourne and resumed his role as the Training Warrant Officer at Regimental HQ. Once more he was at a desk organising the RAAF aircraft and Naval vessels for the essential training regime of the officers and men of the Sabre Squadrons.

'It was a change of pace,' he says. 'No question about that. But it meant that I could see the kids again and become part of their lives as they grew up.' He found a rental townhouse in the Perth suburb of Doubleview where they could come to stay. 'I'd always got along well with Callan but Kelsee was particularly good. When she was 13 she decided for herself that she wanted to spend as much time with me as with her mother. I admired her for that.'

It was at this time that a woman from an earlier time stepped quietly back into his life. 'Debbi Christine Cvitan is a fine woman,' Palmer says. 'I first met her at school in

Kalgoorlie in 1973 and we became good friends. We would chat on the lawns during recess and lunch, and both represented the school in hockey at the Country Week in Perth.

'What I didn't see was what she wanted – and it came to a point where she couldn't wait any longer for me to sort myself out. Arguably, I have missed the golden opportunity to embrace a wonderful person and build a lasting and complete future. She remains very dear to me.'

20

OPERATIONAL SUPPORT
SQUADRON

The January 2010 assignments in the SASR reinforced Palmer's return to the centre of the regimental mainstream. He became sergeant major at Operational Support Squadron, a key position in the development of the regiment. One of his main priorities concerned selection and training of new recruits. 'That was very much in my duty statement,' he says.

As he set about the task he reflected on the way the selection course had developed historically. 'My course [in 1984] was about 23 days,' he says, 'the longest three weeks I'd endured in my military career; it was hard, but all courses were. A few years before my time, they covered a longer period but they probably weren't as intense. They spent a couple of weeks in Perth and then went somewhere else for the patrolling phase; then they went to New Guinea and did another. The whole process took six to eight weeks, and because we were in Vietnam in those days they were rolling in a lot of jungle training stuff.

'But in the years after I did mine they rearranged the selection process, and the basic system was that we get these guys together, we put them through a rigorous testing selection regime and whatever we get out the other end, we start to train up in certain skills; and then if they get through that bit they'll go into a Sabre squadron and they'll become SAS troopers. That's the reinforcement training regime.

'The unit used to send out a team to all different major military bases around the country where the candidates turned up for a physical run test – the two-miler – and if they didn't make a certain time it was "See you later; go back to your unit." The selection course itself was traditionally at Swanbourne and on Rottnest Island. They used to go across there to Kingstown barracks and run it out of there. Then they went over to the army infantry centre in Singleton and used the Pokolbin Valley, but it was too damn cold. So in '84 they shifted it back to Perth base and held it at the army camp up in Northam. They used the Sterling Ranges in the south for the endurance phase and then we had another phase at Bindoon training area.

'But over the years it's become more sophisticated. We wanted to know whether candidates could hack it mentally. We'd say, "Guys, we're going for a run. It's about 8 ks; it should take us about an hour; let's go."

'Well, an hour and 20 minutes later and they're still running, and the guy conducting the exercise is acting normal, keeping going, and they're all thinking, "Shit, where's the finish line? We should have finished already because he told us it would only take about an hour."

'Then they'd see the finish line, "Oh, thank God!" but we'd keep going straight past it. It's like, "It's not fair!" So there was that sort of pressure. Of course, we'd only go another hundred metres and stop. But it was to test the reaction of guys who thought they only had to do enough to get to the end but then had to continue. It's a psychological thing, because if you think you only have to run for any hour, your mind is programmed to say, "That's it, you're finished", and then your body stops. But the endurance test is to keep going, and that sort of thing happened all the time.'

As the combined selection course developed, new elements were added. 'We introduced navigation revision, medical awareness lectures, navigation lectures, radio communication,' he says, 'so it was an environment where you were tested on how much you knew, and also it was consolidation or a revision for those blokes who had done it before. It would get you up to speed when you went out in the field and were left to your own devices. You knew your radio; if you got bitten by a snake you could look after yourself; all that sort of stuff.'

The course was broken up in two phases. The first four or five days, it was a lot of PT and 'getting tortured'; plus minor tactics. Then they tested the candidates ability to write under pressure. The DS would give them two pieces of paper and say, 'Write your life's history down', to assess overall skill level.

'Then there was the teamwork phase, including one night exercise where they had to get up and do things', he says. 'This was particularly tough for the officers. Sleep deprivation was a big one for them; it tested their ability to think and to plan and to lead people under stressful situations; so sleep deprivation came into it quite a bit for all candidates.'

The second phase was the navigational exercises, where they would also introduce an endurance factor. 'They'd have a 24 hour navigation task where they were required to find a number of markers, and there was a cut-off point – if they had more than four they were good; if they had under four, they were in trouble', he says. 'It was all about weeding out the weaker from the stronger.'

Then came the overnight test. 'We'd send them out into the bush to see how they would cope on their own. You'd be surprised how many people freak out in darkness on their own. They're scared of the dark. And there's only kangaroos and lizards and stuff like that. It's Australia! Nothing's going to kill you out there.'

After they graduated from that there was an endurance navigation phase out in the Stirling Ranges. They had five days to do the five peaks. 'Depending on what route you were given, this would determine how good your endurance was, but no matter which route you were given, all included five peaks, and so you had one day, basically, to complete each peak and get to the finish point on day five – that was the cut-off. When I did it there were three of us who made it in two and a half days. Pretty good!'

They were then redeployed to Bindoon for the final phase, which was the endurance teamwork phase, with certain tasks to complete, some of which were apparently not achievable. 'But you know what? They are achievable if you work hard and if you are concentrating and have the guts to do it', he says.

'When I was instructing we used to go and test the tasks. We were fresher, sure, but we'd go out and we'd do it. When you're run down, you're tired, you're pissed off, you've lost weight, and you're not feeling too sharp, it's still doable – and it tests the character of the individual to push him through that part where ordinarily, he'd say, "This is impossible, can't do it."

'It was physically difficult, we all knew that, but there was a way. If you were able to think through the problem, you would eventually come up with the right way to do it, and a lot of people did it. A lot of people couldn't; they just didn't get it, so they didn't actually get through that phase. But all the phases were timed, so no matter how far you got, if you ran out of time, you'd hear, "Okay, stop," and you left for the next task.'

There was not much sleep in the last four days. 'They'd do their day task, after which they were whacked, then they'd have a night task until at least three o'clock in the morning. Then they'd get up at five; two hours sleep are gone and they've been working like mad things because they're carrying their packs, their radios and that's when people start niggling and fighting. It's quite amusing when you're on the outside looking in, but it's quite different when you're going through it, particularly if you're appointed as the leader. Then we'll say, "Okay, Blogs, this is the problem. What are you going to do about it?" As a DS you are deliberately provocative to the point where it sometimes is interpreted as being offensive; they take it personally because they're tired and pissed off and it might be raining or hot as shit. And you really give them a hard time. "Come on, you haven't made a decision yet. Why haven't you made a decision yet? I've given you two minutes. It's not hard, mate. Come on, give me an answer."

'There's a little bit of pressure put on guys at times; there's a little bit of instructor licence there, to put the weights on people, to get them motivated. But then there's the other side of the coin, too, where you've given them the instruction, "Listen carefully, I'm going to give you a brief." Then yap, yap, yap; brief over, "Go!" And you stand back and watch them, and give no feedback – this tactic is just as useful and effective as beasting people.

'The structure of the course has not changed greatly over the years, but the methodology and the psychology behind it has evolved. 'Now, we monitor every individual in far more detail than they used to', he says. 'When I did my course, the directing staff would sit around a table and talk about the candidates. They each had a bit of paper with some notes and they'd come up with decisions.

'But now, in order to give a full and fair picture of an individual, you have to assess him regularly, consistently, and by many people. So you get that cross-pollination of interpretations from all those people over an extended period of time, under all those different conditions. There's a red, amber, and a green sort of thing; so if he's doing badly or he fails something, he gets a red and a word picture. If he's an on-the-fence guy, he gets an amber mark but he also gets a word picture because you've got to justify the red, amber, or green by a statement to say why. If he gets a tick of green, you also say why he was good.

'We can't afford to rob the candidate of the best possible chance for him to get through. This is not about you getting rid of him and protecting your own position or unit. This is about selecting the future of our unit. So you need to afford them the best possible opportunity to prove themselves, and you can only do that fairly if you spend time looking at them in all sorts of conditions.

'We try to use as many directing staff as we can and they rotate too, on different activities. I will be on an activity and all these blokes will pass through so I will see all of them. There are some days that we're floating around, and as floaters we'll go from activity to activity; some only see people twice; sometimes they wouldn't see people at all. But the deal is that on a daily basis all the assessments that I and the other instructors make would go back to the main centre and would be compiled onto the databases. So, at the end of every day, the boss would go, "Right, so we have an updated version every day of how the candidates are going", and it was colour-coded red, amber or green so he'd get a clear indication of how things were going.'

At the end of each major phase, or periodically through the course, there would be a board of studies of all the senior people involved in the selection process, to go through every single person and assess their progress. 'We decided whether we should withdraw people because of their poor performance or whether we should say, "He's borderline so we should let him go a bit further. If he does well in the next phase, we'll take him on; he's trainable. Otherwise, you're out, dude."

'You don't compromise on the numbers or in any other way, not even if the candidate is your best mate and a good guy. But you have to make some tough calls. One particular bloke that comes to mind – a Townsville-based soldier – did the selection course three times. He physically made it through every time, but there was always one thing at the end of it that made him not suitable. And it broke his heart. Great guy, good soldier, but just didn't have that little bit extra that was needed to get him over the line. It was probably more personality-based because he was a quiet guy; he probably didn't have enough mongrel in him to project himself in a way that people would want him in the team. It's one of those strange things; there's a little bit of subjectivity about it, you know? Because in those days, the bottom line was, "Would you have him in your patrol?" And more people said no than yes, I guess.

'To alleviate the politics of that sort of thing, we came up with this system that was still an interpretation by the DS to write him up subjectively, if he wanted to, but if he did that, against the others that were objective, then that would stand out, so therefore it's a balance. It's a quality control check on the assessor as well. You have to be open-minded and objective about what you see. You've got to do it the right way.'

Leadership qualities were important. 'When a young soldier comes to the course he's got at least three years' experience in an infantry battalion. He might have gone to Afghanistan already, and have battle experience; he knows what it's all about. You aren't going to muck him around; you're going to treat him like a man, like one of the guys. Some of these diggers who have got that sort of experience come through with flying colours and they already have leadership ability. So they do shine on many occasions and they outshine some of the guys who have the rank on their arms – the corporals, the sergeants, and sometimes even the officers who are really lacking in the leadership stakes.

'Being a lieutenant or a captain in some nebulous unit out there in the wider army – that's not a testing time for you, because you only need to keep your nose clean for the next two years and you're promoted to the next rank, then fours year after to the next rank, and six years later, and so it goes. But when you're under the pump, when you really have to show your mettle and you're putting yourself on display, trying to convince the members of the SAS Regiment that you're good enough to break into the ranks, and that you really are a leader, that's when quality counts.

'It's particularly important because when a captain comes in he goes straight to being a troop commander, whereas soldiers come in at bottom level, as troopers. They might have worked their way up to corporal or sergeant, but then do selection course, relinquish the rank, and come back to trooper.

'Lieutenants aren't eligible. We only take captains. If you make it through selection, you do probably two or three years at the regiment so that chews up three years of your captain time. Then you have to go and do a staff job somewhere because they have things mapped out in a normal officer career continuum. That's why they don't relinquish rank. But they are under the pump because we expect more of officers. We expect more of leaders. People who are already designated leaders, we expect them not to dwindle and drop away, but to step up even further, even higher, because even in the SAS you need a good, strong leader. And if you don't have a good, strong troop commander, the boys are going to run all over the top of you because the boys are hard, they're smart, and they don't take shit.

'On the course, they're all candidates; they're all equal. As a warrant officer I'd never call the officers "Sir" because that psychologically means that I'm subordinate to them. My attitude – and it's the same for all the DS – is "You are a candidate on this selection course. I will tell you what's going on here. I am in control. I'm telling you, if you want to make the grade, you have got to do what you're told." That's never intimidated me at all. I'd been doing selection courses on and off for years. Even when I was a young trooper, I helped out on the selection course. I was a DS on selection when [a future] CO was a young captain at the time. I was a corporal and I gave him a hard time; and within a few months, he became my troop commander. I don't think he ever forgave me but he brought it up one day over a few beers and had a little chuckle about it. "You prick, you had to," he said. And I said, "Oh, yeah, but it was all worth it, wasn't it?"'

The exchange highlights not just the camaraderie of the SASR, but also the changing nature of power and influence exercised within the regiment. When he first came into the unit, Palmer says, there was 'something of a power struggle' between the senior NCOs and the officer corps. 'I remember the warrant officer Mafia, as it was called,' he says. 'There was a bit of skullduggery going on between certain personalities on a number of occasions. But the reality is that officers are put in command and the senior NCOs and the warrant officers conduct the training on the behalf of the commanders. That's how it's structured. That's how it should be. But then you get the old, crusty warrant officer who seems to think that these young officers come to the place as self-serving and for their own career benefit, so stuff them. "They don't come here and mess with what we've made. We've been here for 20 years."

'Over the years we've got a lot better in handling that and particularly when we became involved in operational tasking. It became more than obvious then that we had to rely on each other equally and that to be a good officer, you had to understand and know your men, and work well beside them.

'The troop commander is a captain. There's only one captain in the troop, and he commands three or four patrols. The patrol leaders are normally sergeants; and if there's no sergeant, there's a senior corporal who will step up and be patrol commander. If you take the captain out of the troop headquarters environment and put him as the patrol commander, that gives him two jobs to do. And the patrol commander's job is a really demanding one. So that's to be avoided. But certainly the relationship now with the officers in the regiment is far, far closer with the soldiers and the NCOs than it's been for a while.'

21

BOOTS ON THE GROUND

After a year at Swanbourne, Palmer was ready for a deployment back to the action in Afghanistan. In October 2010, his CO Paul Burns obliged with what would become the most responsible appointment of his career. As he flew out of Perth for the Australian HQ at Tarin Kot, he was heading into a conflict that would test every element of the task force and Clint himself to the limit of their capabilities.

Since he left the area in June 2009, the war had taken several turns for the worse and some for the better. President Obama's appointment of General Stanley McChrystal to lead the International Security Assistance Force (ISAF), now dominated by the Americans, had become increasingly controversial. McChrystal had commanded the Special

Forces operations (JSOC) in Iraq for five years from 2003 and was responsible for transforming JSOC into 'a force of unprecedented agility and lethality' with a number of high-profile 'kills' to his credit, including al-Zarqawi, the leader of al-Qaeda in Iraq. But at the same time his men were implicated in the horrors of Abu Ghraib and other abusive interrogation incidents at Camp Nama.

McChrystal took much of the credit for the claimed success of the 'surge' in Iraq; and in 2008 he had returned to Washington to promotion as director of Joint Staff, a powerful position within the Pentagon bureaucracy. It put him at the centre of decisions on troop deployments and the make-up of forces used in military operations. There he joined with other military leaders urging President Obama – against the warnings of Vice-President Joe Biden – to surge US forces in Afghanistan. And, on his appointment there, he warned publicly that 'We face not only a resilient and growing insurgency; there is also a crisis of confidence among Afghans – in both their government and the international community – that undermines our credibility and emboldens the insurgents.'[37]

One of the first operations under his command was Khanjar (Strike of the Sword) in Helmand province, with 4,000 American troops and about 650 Afghans. It was designed to counter Taliban attempts to disrupt the August elections, and the result was the deadliest combat month for Allied forces since 2001. In September he submitted a report to Defence Secretary Robert Gates warning that the war might be lost if more troops weren't sent. However, with a further 30,000 men in the field, 'Success is still achievable.'

By now he was surrounded by his own PR team, and they ensured that the report became public. Two months later he was back in Washington briefly to present his arguments directly to President Obama. By now he had raised the upper level of the surge to 40,000 additional troops.

On 1 December, President Obama backed most of McChrystal's demands with an announcement that another 30,000 troops would be deployed to Afghanistan. It was the high point in the general's career; in a fit of hubris he and his aides boasted about their bureaucratic victory to a *Rolling Stone* reporter, Michael Hastings, and spiced their tales with mocking remarks about Vice-President Biden and the US Ambassador to Afghanistan, Karl Eikenberry.

Publication of the resulting article set off a chain reaction in the White House. McChrystal apologised publicly, admitting it was 'a mistake reflecting poor judgement'. But the damage was done and he was summoned to the Oval Office where in a sharp 20-minute meeting the president accepted his resignation. He would be succeeded by the head of the US Central Command, General David Petraeus, another of the Pentagon high fliers with his own team of PR flaks to raise his personal and political profile. In time, he too would crash to earth in a press scandal,[38] but for the moment his appointment energised the Allied troops. He had taken a step down the promotional ladder to return to the battlefield and was eager to pursue the 'hearts and minds' role in the conflict and raise the profile of the Afghan military and civil authorities.

The deployment of additional US troops continued in early 2010, with 9,000 arriving before the end of March and another 18,000 – mainly from the 101st Airborne Division – by June. The composition of the force meant a sixfold increase in Special Forces overall, and this was reflected in Australia's area of responsibility, the troublesome Oruzgan Province.

The allies stepped up the air war, with more than 700 strikes across the country in September 2010 alone compared with 260 in the whole of 2009. An American body count claimed that between July and October, 300 Taliban commanders and 800 fighters were killed, and the rate of fire was increasing. Petraeus said, 'We've got our teeth in the enemy's jugular now, and we're not going to let go.'[39] At the same time the CIA Counter-terrorism Pursuit Teams expanded their operations from the border provinces into Pakistan itself and scored important 'kill or capture' results, not least with the growing use of unmanned drones.

In Oruzgan the Americans organised a major gathering of the clans – known locally as a 'shura' – to encourage support for the central government. Held in a school that had recently been the hub of insurgent activity in the region, it was dominated by members of the Matakzai who had controlled the eastern part of Khaz Oruzgan, where the combined Australian/American Special Forces group had been ambushed in 2008 in the action that led to Trooper Donaldson's VC.

Palmer arrived on 3 November 2010 at Tarin Kot, a town of about 10,000 people, with some 200 small shops in the city's bazaar. He went directly from the airstrip on the outskirts to the Australian HQ, Camp Russell, named for Andy Russell, who had been killed in action nine years previously. The Americans had built the major installation in 2004 and the Australians had shared an area with the Dutch that was divided into Camp Holland and Camp Russell. Australian soldiers had regularly described it as a 'dusty shit-hole'; however, with constant upgrades and the final withdrawal of the Dutch in August 2010 it now offered a reasonable standard of accommodation and facilities for Task Force Uruzgan. This comprised the provincial reconstruction team, the battle group, the Apache close air support group, the logistical support team and a hospital.

'There were many old buildings still in use,' Palmer says, 'but work was ongoing to make the place a fortress. Tarin Kot was under constant construction, building more permanent structures and hardening the dirt runway. The initial accommodation for us was "B huts", as the Americans called them. They were made of wood with a galvanised iron – very cold in winter and boiling hot in summer. But the bottom line was they weren't bomb-proof so we had hardened accommodation built to satisfy the political pressure on Defence to ensure that every measure possible was taken to protect us.

'The issue of force protection was number one on any agenda. Hence the continuation of big dollars being spent over there. The road system, however, was all dirt, and the volume of traffic was such that dust was a factor 24/7.'

One of the more unusual aspects of the Afghan war was its division into a so-called fighting season followed by a period of apparent inactivity during the depths of winter. The inactivity was more apparent than real, as the insurgents would use it to consolidate their command and control systems, fire up a propaganda campaign, plan operations against the Coalition and, where possible, lay IEDs along strategic routes to be activated once fighting recommenced in earnest.

The allies also used the relative calm to regroup and revise both strategic and tactical approaches to the next phase of the war. However, they would not withdraw from the battlefield completely. While the main body of the Special Operations Task Group drew down, according to Palmer, 'A group was tasked with keeping a finger on the pulse.' And over Christmas/New Year 2010–11 he was put in charge. 'I was OC of the drawdown team,' he says. For the first time since Operation Anaconda, WO Palmer was returning to the battlefield.

It was a firm vote of confidence. While most of his time would be spent training his partner force, the Provincial Response Company, an arm of the Afghan Police Force, he would also lead his men on patrol outside Tarin Kot. 'We needed to keep them up to speed with their skill sets,' he says. 'So when our main field element came back in the spring to start the fighting season, the Afghans had maintained their skill level to re-join them on the battlefield.'

His unit consisted of six SAS soldiers, and they had their hands full in dealing with between 80 and 120 Afghans. 'They had some sense of unity and purpose,' Clint says. 'They were well led by Afghan standards and some had a good idea of what it was all about; others had no idea at all. This is the sort of thing you're up against. You have to make judgements about the quality of the people you're dealing with. You have to absorb all that and deal with a language barrier, a cultural barrier and an intellectual barrier. And from personal experience spending weeks with these guys teaching them basic stuff, some of them still could not do it at the end of that time.'

The forces were usually separated in the evenings. 'We lived in our garrison and they lived in their garrison down the road, and they would come to us every day,' he says. 'The training was basic weapons handling skills, shooting, basic formation movement, fire and manoeuvre. We worked on their fitness, endurance and training. We fed them our food. And the food was great there; it catered for both Western and Afghan tastes. They loved it because soft drink and ice-cream in the fridge is a big deal for them. Afghans usually have fruit as a dessert and they loved fruit, especially bananas. When a shipment arrived they would sit at the table with a box of bananas and eat them, then fill their pockets with bananas and go out and eat them too. They loved them.

'They're peculiar blokes. Their uniforms were grey/blue pants with shirt and top pockets and a cap. We had a training complex down the back where we would train them to a minimal standard that was compatible with our guys. And we did night training as well.'

He was greatly assisted by the high quality of his SAS colleagues. 'We selected our guys on the basis of experience and availability,' he says. 'They were well trained, smart, hard, and when they go over there they know they will have to work with a percentage of Afghans. A third of the complete force had to be locals, so they know how important it is to have them up to speed. And that ratio would change to 50 per cent before handover. Most Australian soldiers are trainers; that's what they do: raise, train, sustain; and it's a perpetual thing. So I had great support from our guys.'

Part of his task was to coordinate the operations of his unit – FE Alpha – with the Reserve Commandos (CDO) from NSW and Victoria who were doing a four-month deployment over the winter. 'Their task was to maintain low-level engagement with the Taliban and insurgents in order to maintain a feel for the battlespace and keep in tune with what was going on in the area of operations,' he says. 'CDO would go out into the field and conduct operations. It was important to be seen and to be filling the battlespace with low-level engagements. And our people became involved in that after a while, so it became one big group in the field.'

One reason for Palmer's team taking part was the partnering ratio. 'They needed extra bodies to fill the ratio of Australians versus Afghans,' he says. 'If they didn't take our guys on board they wouldn't have sufficient numbers to complete the task the way they wanted to.

'If you take three or four extra Australians, you've got an extra couple of Afghans as well – that gives you an extra six or eight people on the ground. So we started to work with CDO, and this meant the winter team comprised two parts: my team and CDO team at company strength.

'This was useful because we got the boys out and about, and at the same time we were meeting our training obligations to our partnering force. Most of these operations with CDO were only short – out in the morning, back that day – but some were three or four days and the longest seven days to 10 days.'

Once in the field they had to be on high alert. The insurgents might not be out in strength but the threat of contact was ever present. 'We did a clearing task in a place called Zamberay in a valley,' he says. 'It was a three-day operation to get boots on the ground and clear the valley, because there were signs of insurgent movement heading towards a larger system. So we went out. There were a number of areas of interest in that valley – in the village system, for example, there had been some suspicious activity so we went to see if there was a weapons cache.

'We figured there might be a centre where the bad guys were bringing things to or taking things from. The activity was detected from all sources – technological and humint, where people come in and say, "Come and help us; bad guys are coming in at night and scaring us." We put it all together and in the overall scheme of things it builds a picture. So you go out there and see what they're up to. It was a relatively low-level operation, but we knew there were characters out there worthy of note. So we went out to have a look.'

The CO of the task group in Tarin Kot as in charge of the operation in Afghanistan, with the chain of command rising through the Australian commander in theatre in the Middle East, and then back to Australia. On the ground, the officer in command of the commandos was running the operation. Clint was with his own team, blistered on to one of the platoons.

'There were two waves going out,' he says. 'We had a Black Hawk helicopter, about 60 of us and another 30 Afghans. But this was a big area – 6 or 7 kilometres long and a kilometre across. I was in the second lift out to the landing zone,' he says. 'We secured the LZ, picked up one bad guy who saw us coming, ran away and threw his gun in the water and said, "No, not mine."

'This was the normal thing they do. So we got him, back-loaded him, and then cleared an area some distance from the helipad, maybe three or four hundred metres. Nothing serious to report; but one of the compounds that was of interest was further up the valley. It was probably an acre in area. You might find one family in it, or a bloke might have two wives and several kids as well as his cousins. There could be up to 10 or 12 people living in a compound.

'They're basically designed to house the people, their animals and their goods and chattels. The big walls are there to keep things in and keep things out. So during winter the billy goats or dogs or their cow will come into the compound. They're designed to sustain life over the winter. Sometimes they even keep them in tunnels under the ground to shelter them from the winter snows. But during the better months they'll take the animals out to feed them and keep them in separate pens or compounds. The buildings are sometimes on two levels with a parapet around the top. They can be quite intricate, but most are pretty basic with mud walls.

'We were on our way – myself and another SAS operator and half a dozen locals from our partnering force and our interpreter. We were patrolling up towards this compound and we heard chatter on the ICOM [radios], and we saw movement up to our left on the high ground, about 200 metres away. There were three or four figures in chest harness. Then we heard chatter: "Will we shoot them now or wait till they come out in the open? They're all down the creek. No, we'll wait here until they move out and hit them with the big gun . . ." all this sort of stuff.

'At that stage we'd also heard that there were six or seven bad guys moving from further up the valley down towards us. So we were moving up, knowing that up the valley about a kilometre away there were these others coming down our way. We could only assume that a group that size was trouble. Farmers or normal people don't move in a group that size, especially when they're fighting-age males (FAMs).'

22

AFGHAN NEGOTIATIONS

I t was 3.30 in the afternoon. The farmers and the villagers at that time of day are invariably still out with their sheep or goats or up in an enclave among the rocks for the night where they light a fire for warmth. The shepherds remain with their flocks and bring them back to the compound the next day. Normally it's a job for young boys between eight and 14. So Palmer and his team were deeply suspicious when they spotted adult males on the hillside with a flock of sheep. 'Sometimes you get these older people apparently looking after the sheep, but they're not just shepherds,' he says. 'Their weapons would be stowed up in the rocks or hills somewhere.

'So we went down into the creek bed, which was about 10 metres wide with a bank on one side about a metre high.

We were sitting down behind the ledge, looking out. The main group that we left had snipers up on the high ground some distance away. They could see across the valley and pick up the position where these characters were sitting. Once they spotted them it was decided through the chain of command that we would continue to move and the contact with these guys would be initiated by the sniper team. When the snipers opened up on them we could also return fire and move out of the creek.

'Another group of seven or eight insurgents were still a couple of kilometres away, still moving towards us. My offsider wanted to move, but I said, "Look, if you do that you're out in the open. We don't have the support yet so just hang there." And we radioed back to the group we'd just left and said, "Send up another patrol." So they came up in support. After they arrived, the sniper team initiated contact. So we had two elements on the ground and we could fire and move out of our position.

'It suddenly got very noisy. Our partnering force thought that was the signal to just open up. And, of course, they all did, and they started unloading on these three guys up on the hill. They didn't know what hit them. Then they started shooting down on us.

'Initially when the snipers opened up, the first shot missed and hit the rock behind the bad guy's head and a shard of rock flew back and hit him. It was about a 900-metre shot.

When we captured him a bit later, he had this huge laceration on the side of his forehead. We had killed one of them and wounded two.

'After the shooting died down, we moved on to clear the compound. When we reached it the people had all gone inside to hide. We called them out. They were very nervous but we asked them the usual questions, and they said, "No Taliban, no Taliban", and we let them go. There was nothing in it of interest. You know what you're looking for. You know the little old farmer, fingers all gnarled, hands rough as guts, his wife and a couple of kids – no threatening FAMs in the compound 'cause they're all out and about. So you leave them be.

'At the same time that was happening, elements from the rest of the company were dispatched on to the high ground to do a sweep through the area, and as a consequence of that, just before last light, the group up on the high ground to the rear came across these other chaps who'd been moving down the valley towards us. It turned out there were four of them. They had a contact, bowled over the first guy; a couple of others disappeared, but by then it was dark and they couldn't exploit it. So they stayed in position overnight.

'At first light this group got up, found the blood trails, and followed them to a guy with his leg badly wounded. He was still alive so they patched him up and brought him down. We sent another team up to where we were the day before, but up the hill. And they came across the other guys.

'Here's the thing – that old fella with the kids in the compound – that was his son up on the hill, badly wounded. He was 20 years old . . . a bad boy. There was another one who'd stayed with him through the night. So we sent all three back and they were processed at Tarin Kot.'

That night they remained on patrol. 'We had our normal sleeping bags but it was very cold,' he says. 'If we found an abandoned compound we'd move in. But on this occasion it was occupied and we had to commandeer it. We paid them a few dollars – they wanted Pakistani money – and I ended up with another bloke in a donkey's feedlot for the night.

'That was a long day, and later that night I was on duty. So that was Zamberay, New Years Eve 2010.' He laughs, 'I was 53 years 10 months and six or seven days old, and I thought to myself, "What the hell am I doin' here? I shouldn't be doin' this stuff at my age. This is bullshit. I'm outta here."'

Next morning they continued the sweep. 'There were at least seven bad guys in that particular area, plus the one we caught when the boys went in,' he says. 'In other compounds there were three or four FAMs between 17 and 35. They're in regular clothes, just squatting down watching you.

'Funnily enough, the next day when we did the sweep through we found one of these young fellows in a crack in the rocks. He saw us coming and tried to hide. We pulled him out and there in a far corner was a Kalashnikov. The place is crawling with them. But they see us with 20 or 30 Afghan police and they're too scared to do anything. So they just wait for an opportune time to open up on us.

'It turned out these guys were not all from the area. One guy had the Taliban black turban, the vest and the weapon. He occupied a compound with his wife right on the edge of the village area – a place where transients could easily move through. He was a person who would accommodate other Taliban, feed them then send them on their way.

'This was the pattern – as they moved through they would have safe houses in certain villages and the resident Taliban or insurgent guy would be the heavy-handed dude who would keep the safe house open for them by intimidating the locals. He would have his weapon with him all the time. As soon as the Coalition was coming he'd hide it somewhere, and when they left he'd pull it out again and he would control the area.

'These were the guys we were after.'

Palmer's drawdown deployment ended on 17 February 2011, when he took a brief and well-deserved leave home to Perth. He had happy reunions with Callan and Kelsee. 'They were short meetings, for lunch or coffee,' he says. 'I spent most of my leave attending to my father, who I noticed had lost a significant amount of weight since I had left. I took him to doctors, specialists and then had to organise home care for him before I returned. I had no time to relax or even go to the movies; all my time was spent with him. I finished setting up his care package at 1930 the evening prior to going back to Afghanistan on 1 March. I'd had one night spare to be with my family, and we all went to dinner – including Kimalee – at a small local cafe. By the time I got back to start work on 3 March, I was knackered.'

It was no way to begin the most responsible and demanding job of his career. For the next six months he would be the man in the middle, liaising with the Afghan authorities before every mission undertaken by Australia's Special Forces. He stepped straight into the task. 'My job was at the operational coordination centre-provincial (OCC-P),' he says, 'so it was the conduit between what Special Operations Task Group (SOTG) and the Afghan provincial authorities to coordinate operations in the TK bowl as well as the greater provincial area of Oruzgan. The guidelines for operating the partnership with the Afghans meant we had to seek approval from the local authorities to conduct operations in Oruzgan. It was a very, very sensitive juggling act,' he says.

The main issue was the timing of briefings to the Afghans – when the Coalition sought their authority to conduct the operation and when it was actually conducted. 'Obviously, the security aspects and the sensitivity of certain missions were paramount and could be jeopardised with the more time they had to leak,' he says. 'So the idea was to seek approval for the operation just as the operation was launched. And my job was essentially to liaise directly with the provincial governor, whose name was Ishmael Sherzad – he was related to [President] Karzai.'

Palmer found him an interesting character. 'He'd lost his left arm in conflict against the Russians,' he says, 'He was a big man, 6 foot 4, and tough with it. He understood English very well – quite good for an Afghan – but he chose to speak in his own language through an interpreter. He was basically stamping his authority as an Afghan. He was saying "I am an Afghan; I speak in my tongue, thank you, and you will take what I say through an interpreter". In the main they were educated in America and had very American accents.

'So on a daily basis I was liaising with him; and in the absence of the provincial governor I would deal directly with the chief of police. He was the man who basically worked side by side with the governor in law and order issues within the province and was also seen as an alternative authority for us to conduct operations.

'The deputy governor was also a man who we would talk to in the absence of the governor. He was an older gentleman, a tribal elder, and he was very much a camp follower, a puppet, and wasn't that smart, probably not as educated as the governor. So we'd meet the governor and cover the concept of operations for the ensuing month or so.'

The 'concept' was a generalised plan for a series of operations designed to stabilise an area or respond to insurgent activity. 'We had a number of operations that were open at the same time, but they had different tasks,' Palmer says. 'Some were confined to reconnaissance, others were looking for specific people, so there were all different types of operation, and each different type had its own name. I would have to brief the concept of the operation to the governor to get approval.

'Then it would go up to HQ ISAF to get approval. The CO SOTG would then have to go to the Special Forces commander of ops in Kandahar; they would then have to present it to the Special Forces operation chain in Bagram; and that would have to come back signed off. The operation would not launch until all that was done.

'All the information in the document would be translated into Dari, the local language, by my interpreter. And once it was all written up in their language (in a version that we were happy to release) I would then take the master document plus a copy to the governor and have them both signed, give the governor his copy, and make sure our copy was kept in our records. If we needed to refer back to the Operation, we'd have all the paperwork complete.'

Though it was time-consuming, the process was relatively simple to administer. 'We had to get mission approval for each mission we launched on each day of the operation. So in a prolonged operation over three weeks we would have quite a number of separate mission tasks and as that occurred

I had to get specific authority to conduct each particular mission under the umbrella of the larger operation. So I was working 18 hours a day every day.'

Once in operation, the system worked well. 'The Americans who were working the same area didn't have to do it because they weren't working for ISAF. They were working under OEF (Operation Enduring Freedom) so they had different rules. But we had to toe the party line on a daily basis.'

There were times when the Afghan authorities were not prepared to approve the operations. 'A couple of times they said, "No"', Palmer says. 'They'd use any excuse; they might claim they were doing an operation in the same area and suggest we talk so we could deconflict. That was pretty standard – if the police were there at the same time there'd have to be a line of deconfliction. I would have to know where they were so I could tell our force to ensure that we didn't clash with them.

'I would have to go down to the OCC-P every time and brief them so they would be aware of what was going on. That was the central question for the Afghan forces – to know where we were.' This brought frustrations on both sides and he says required all his tact and diplomacy.

'Thankfully any interference or speed humps we had were minimal,' he says. 'I managed to get a good rapport with these people. Often we would do our business then we would just have a talk. I built a good friendship with some of them.' This was particularly valuable since the Afghans generally remained in their posts for extended periods. 'The personnel changed only when they were assassinated or blown up in a car bomb,' he says.

The governor and his team were themselves having to juggle obligations to both the Coalition and the villagers. 'Within the province each large town would have areas around it with their own domains,' he says. 'They would be represented by a head man of the village, and he would come to TK and talk to the governor if there were issues in that particular area. There was quite an extensive network of those people, and the governor would listen to them depending on what side of the fence they sat – whether they were pro-Karzai or pro-insurgent.

'So there was all that politics. But what I also found over time was that if they were briefed we were going in on a certain day a week later, for instance, they would often come up with "local intelligence" that would mean we couldn't go in that day; instead it would be a couple of days later.

'I'd ask, "Why is that?" and they'd make up some excuse, but it was to let the bad guys out before our team went in. They'd be talking to the Taliban quite often, but of course they'd deny it. "Oh no," they'd say, "No, no, no, Taliban no good."'

'This was double-edged, obviously; we'd tell our own intelligence agencies and systems. But sometimes they'd miss something that was localised and I'd be able to pick up information through the OCC-P. The police were very good at feeding information, but sometimes they'd also feed misinformation, so if anything peculiar or different from what we knew came up I would obviously pass it straight back to our information people and they would either know about it already or go, "Oh shit", and start putting the feelers out on their networks. And the picture would develop from that information.

'But in the main we were fairly sweet about the information we had anyway, and it was all in line to complement our operation. But we also had to fit in with the locals who had the authority. This meant we stayed very much in step with them because we couldn't afford to blot the copybook, as it were.

'We had many occasions when the locals would be pissed off. "Why do you come here and kill all these innocent people?" Our response would be, "Well, we have information that they are not so innocent."

'"No, that's wrong information". It turns out they're on the take; they all are.

'Sometimes we'd have these crisis management meetings. I'd get a phone call from the governor: "What the fuck is going on? I want you to please explain!" So I'd go to the boss. We'd have to go into town and smooth things over. Many times we were there and the CO is getting grilled by the governor in his residence and the boss is trying to explain. And sometimes I'd have to step in and take the heat off him. I'd say, "I briefed so-and-so and they should have briefed you, Governor."

'What a process. After six months it nearly did my head in. Of course, a lot of the problems were caused by the poppy.'

23

THE POPPY

Afghanistan is the world's biggest illicit opium producer, and the export of its principal derivative – heroin – has increased every year of the American occupation. In 2013, the UN's top counter-narcotics official in Kabul, Jean-Luc Lemahieu, said, 'Last year Afghanistan accounted for 75 per cent of the world's heroin supply. The assumption is it will reach again to 90 per cent this year.' And despite the United States' leadership of the so-called 'war on drugs', America remains the biggest illicit importer and consumer of the drug. Moreover, Afghanistan's descent to becoming the world's first true narco-state can be traced to the enthusiastic support given by the CIA to the drug trade's major controllers, the Mujahideen warlords, during the Soviet invasion in the decade from 1979. By 2001 most farmers had switched to poppy growing, and the Karzai Government was soon riddled with corrupt drug lords. Nine years later when Clint took up his liaison posting, the drug trade was protected by both the Karzai Government and the Taliban, which used the income to fund its insurgency.

This bizarre background to the conflict was part of a complex obstacle course Palmer had to negotiate in his key role in Oruzgan. 'The poppy industry is the lifeblood of the country – there's no doubt about that,' he says, 'and Oruzgan is quite a prolific producer because you've got the Kajakai Dam and the river system running into Helmand and straight down to the intersection of Pakistan and Iran in the south-west corner of the country. That was the lifeblood, and the ratlines would run down that way. That's why there was so much fighting in Helmand. They're dug in there and they're fighting fiercely to maintain it. The heroin trade – the resin and the opium – is huge.'

Nevertheless, the ISAF mission was required to at least pay lip service to an 'eradication' program. 'In fact, there are operations underway now – and there have been for a few years – in the eradication of poppies,' Palmer says. 'Of course, they work in close cooperation with the local authorities, so you can only go in at certain times to certain places and destroy a small percentage of the crops. But it has to be seen globally that the effort in Afghanistan is total. It's not just fighting, not just building new infrastructure, it's also taking steps to eradicate the drug trade.

'This is not a job for the SOTG and we weren't doing that. But the Coalition is involved and it's mainly thrown on the shoulders of the local authorities – the police and their own drug enforcement agencies. The police would go in. They'd make the big announcement: "Today we are burning poppies here." It would be a token two acres of the 400,000 acres. But they'd take the TV camera out to show the police were out burning the poppies and declare, "We are fighting the drug problem."

'The SAS didn't ignore it. We fully understood what was going on because the bad guys that we were after were also running the drugs. We weren't targeting the drug aspect specifically – we were targeting the people who were using the drug trade to finance their insurgency. That's the correlation between the two. Sometimes the boys would come across laboratories in certain areas when they went to do a clearance. If they found one, they'd blow it up. But it was all very sensitive and all very diplomatically aligned with protocols.'

While it was a serious complication in Palmer's liaison work, his priorities were clear. Above all, he had to ensure that the provincial Afghan authorities cooperated with the Coalition forces and gave the green light to their operations. 'I had to be totally cognisant of the [Australian] commander's intent,' he says. 'I was the instrument by which he would gain that local authority. So I was the person who had to befriend these people and gain their confidence so that when they got a phone call from me, they could be confident we were doing the right thing and it was all good to go. That's what made the engagement between the two sides so challenging.'

He recalls many occasions when it was necessary to suspend disbelief. 'One time the boss and I went to town to meet the governor about something,' he says. 'We got there and someone came out of his office and said, "Oh sorry, the governor's in a meeting and something's happened and he's dealing with this problem right now. Can you wait upstairs in the tea room?"

'"Certainly."

'They brought chai. It was Nesh, the time when they're harvesting the poppies and collecting all the resin. Of course the governor in previous briefings had said, "Oh no, we don't condone drugs in the area." But when we go upstairs then out on the balcony and look down – in the governor's backyard all the guys are harvesting the poppies, right there in the governor's backyard. At the same time he's signing the authority to go and get these guys, burn the poppies . . .

'Very frustrating, but that's just part of the atmospherics. You sucked it up, dealt with it. We're here to do a job, so we just go and do it and we go along with it because at the highest levels the political rhetoric was that we were aiming at an exit date; there was a strategy in place; we were building on that strategy to posture the ANA and the Afghan forces to take over responsibility for their own security. So, don't worry about being worried; just do what you're told to do.

'In the end I really got to like the job. I knew that what I was doing was the lifeblood of our operation because we could not launch our missions until I got the authority. So it was a very important part of the big picture.'

Another little known complication was that the SOTG were not partnered with the ANA, but the Provincial Police Ready Reaction Auxiliary Force. 'They were a local militia police unit,' Palmer says. 'Afghan National Security Forces is made up of the ANA, the Afghan National Police (ANP) and the Auxiliary Police. The army have their reserves; the police equivalent is known as their auxiliary. The ANA was partnered with the Infantry Battalions MTF (Mentoring Task Force), not us. They would have the ANA embedded there at a ratio that satisfied the partnering document.

'Our working with the police evolved by chance, I suppose,' he says. 'At the time when the partnering aspect came into play, the force that was available and of best advantage to us was the local police in the area.'

At the staff officer level, cooperation between the various units worked relatively well. 'Blistered on within the structure were other specialist groups like 2 Commando Regiment, combat engineers who did the clearances of the IEDs and that sort of thing,' he says. 'There were a number of other people who drove the Bushmaster vehicles – elements from armoured corps or transport people who were Bushmaster qualified – as well as all the administrative and operational staff, intelligence people. And we also had people dedicated to training our partnering force because that was part of our mandate – to train them up to an acceptable standard in order for them to be able to work with our blokes; so if we were relying on these guys in combat we understood their capabilities.

'Most of the time when a concept of operation was briefed, the various elements worked in concert. They might have separate tasking but they would be within the same operation. The SAS would have a task; the commando group would have a separate task. Sometimes they'd be close by, sometimes they'd be very close together, but invariably they'd operate independently.

'For instance if the SAS guys went into a certain place on some reconnaissance task, the information they'd gather might mean that the commandos would then go in and do the job.

'So there were all those sorts of machinations under the one umbrella of the group.'

However, when dealing with the Afghans strict precautions were taken. 'I wouldn't tell the governor what the SAS guys were doing – only the broad operation of the SOTG,' Clint says. 'We tried not to be too specific – things like "time, place, who" we tried to be a little more generic on, although the timing and the date had to be accurate for deconfliction reasons. We would endeavour to brief at the very last moment so they couldn't ring up their mates and tell them to leave because our guys were coming.'

But while dealing with the Afghans was mentally and psychologically testing, there were compensations. Palmer developed a very good relationship with his top-level interpreter.

'He was a very smart bloke,' he says. 'He could interpret from English back to his native tongue, which was Dari. He could read it and write it, so not only would he be able to interpret a conversation, but he'd be able to write it down, thinking it in English or write it down thinking in Dari and writing in English.

'He came from a well-to-do family in Kabul. His father was a businessman and a dentist while his mother was a school teacher, and when the Taliban took over, there was a significant event in Kabul where 700 rockets were launched into the city and a couple of them hit his family's house and demolished it. So he, his brother, his sister, and his parents fled the country into Pakistan. He was 19 at that point. He'd gone to high school in Kabul and he'd started college, but in Pakistan they were refugees for two to three years until they were relocated to the United States.

'His brother went on to college there and is now a gynaecologist in Geneva, so he's a smart cookie as well. He went on to work for the US Government in a number of different areas using his language skills – mostly in Europe and the Middle East – and ended up taking the option of interpreter for the military in Afghanistan. It was his way of giving something back to the country and helping out the Coalition, I suppose. Then he contracted as an interpreter for the American Special Forces for three or four years from the time the Americans went into Afghanistan in 2001. He took a break before coming back with us.

'He came to the camp before I took on the job, and he was working in the headquarters with a very high level of security. He helped us out immensely with some sticky political situations on a number of occasions to get authorisation for certain operations. He understood exactly what the situation was. He had a good feel for atmosphere and he understood what the intent was and he was able to ad lib to win over the confidence of the guy that we were targeting. He was a great guy, a great asset to the team.'

Palmer's liaison role involved working with the several Coalition elements in Uruzgan to coordinate their activities. 'My boss was the head of SOTG, not necessarily the SAS commander, though it could be,' he says. 'Both the SAS and the commandos would have their OC, and those two guys would work to the colonel SOTG, who might be an SAS guy or a commando guy. They would rotate. Normally the SOTG boss would only be there for six months.'

The regular infantry battalion HQ was at Tarin Kot, but their companies would be out dispersed among the Patrol Bases. The SOTG personnel would sometimes go to the Patrol Bases as part of their final preparations for an operation. 'We would cooperate with the infantry guys,' he says, and sometimes incorporate use of the patrol bases in our missions.

'We'd do all our coordination and deconfliction with them, knowing that they have their own patrolling regime from the patrol base. But we'd deconflict so there was no "blue-on-blue".'

However, working with the Afghan forces became increasingly troubled with the rise of Afghan attacks on Coalition soldiers, the so-called 'green-on-blue' incidents. While in 2008 there were only two such attacks, there were five in each of the two succeeding years.

'There was only one on Australians while I was there,' Palmer says. 'LCPC Andrew Jones was killed on 30 May 2011 at Chora – shot dead by a rogue ANA soldier who then jumped the fence and fled! He was found and killed two weeks later.

'The ANA brigade commander had an office right next to our base,' he says. 'He was an interesting character – obviously traumatised by the many years of conflict. He had been captured by the Russians and imprisoned for two years, then spent considerable time in Pakistan before returning to Afghanistan and eventually being promoted to brigadier-general. I sat through his demented fits of rage during conferences and briefings where he would rant and rave about subjects completely unrelated to current ops, and grandstand himself as some kind of VIP. He saw himself as the military commander of the province and therefore thought that the authority for a military operation should come through him. But from our point of view he wasn't the person to give us authority to operate because he had no provincial jurisdiction.

'We steered away from him. The reason he was so upset is because he was responsible for the manning of the OCC-P. And because the OCC-P was under his jurisdiction, he thought he was the authority to approve operations. But he wasn't and we'd have these weekly meetings and he'd get up on his high horse and the governor would have to say, "No". But it would take two hours because the commander of the Coalition forces of TK camp was there. It was all political much of the time, but those touchy feely things were necessary to build the all-important rapport.'

The meetings also frequently involved complaints from villagers in the area to the governor and his aides. 'These guys would get up and say I had all these people coming into my office and complaining that Coalition soldiers had come into the village and were raping women and killing kids,' Palmer says. At such times he would refer to his meticulously kept records. 'I'd point out that we weren't even there at the time,' he says. 'I'd show them: "Here's the record of where we actually were." It was all about trying to get compensation.'

Many of the incidents were to do with deconfliction. The Afghans would complain that they were unaware that Australian forces were in a particular area. 'They'd say, "We didn't know there were people in this place – what were they doing there?" I'd have to explain they were conducting Operation X "which you gave approval to yesterday".

'"I don't remember that."

'"Well, sorry, Sir, I have a document here – do you recall a phone call from my man saying . . ."

'"I don't remember that."

'"Well, I can assure you that you did give the approval and that the appropriate steps have been taken to have the operation authorised and we're very sorry if there's been a misunderstanding. We will rectify the problem as soon as we can." '

One particular incident stands out in his memory. 'There was a high-ranking police auxiliary officer who was a person of interest in the bigger picture,' he says, 'and one of our cordon and search operations included his compound. So of course it was shock horror when the boys entered his place at 4.30 in the morning and searched the joint. His wives and kids were herded into a courtyard or a room and they searched the property for specific items that they suspected might have been located there – weapons, money, harbouring a person – and this police officer goes to his boss [the chief of police] protesting.

'So the chief says he'll talk to us. He tells us, "We're not working with you today since you went to this bloke's compound. He's a good guy, not a bad guy, so why are you searching his compound?"

It was a perennial problem. 'At any level in Afghanistan, people are on the take, including policemen, because they're just Afghanis like everybody else', he says. 'They have to make a living. But they'll front you and lie through their teeth. They'll eyeball you and tell you, "No, I'm not a Taliban, I'm straight; I'm a good guy", whereas in actual fact he's doing deals with people – he's a bad guy. His brother is a Taliban, for example, so he has to show allegiance to his brother and his family members. He has to do this shit because as a policeman they're relying on him to get passageway through an area or whatever and they want protection from him.

'The fact that we may have gained some information about him when we've searched his place is bad for him. So he's complaining, "What do you mean searching my place; you're just a bunch of arseholes." And that puts the brakes on our operations. There was one particular guy whose compound came up time and time again; so we went there time and time again – obviously to get the message through that "You are dealing with the wrong people. If you don't want your compound searched stop dealing with the bad guys."'

On other occasions the SOTG patrol would go to a compound and their partnering force would refuse to enter. Or once they did, there would be a dispute about the Koran. 'That was a tough one,' Clint says. 'You'd search a place and they'd have their Koran wrapped up and you'd push it aside without knowing and there'd be a huge outcry. Very frustrating.'

24

OSAMA BIN LADEN GOES DOWN

The five months Palmer served in the liaison role was during one of the most active and decisive periods of the war. With their 30,000 additional troops on the ground, the Americans began a series of sweeps in March 2011 through known Taliban areas, particularly in the south-east. Their mission was to discover and destroy weapons caches and to disrupt the insurgents' preparations for the spring offensive. The Taliban responded aggressively and towards the end of the month engaged in a battle with units of the US 101st Airborne Division that spilled over into the first week of April. According to the Americans, more than 130 enemy fighters were killed at a cost of only six US soldiers.

Defence Secretary Robert Gates said the surge was clearly having an effect, but he expected combat activity to increase. 'We're still kind of in the middle of the poppy harvest,' he said. 'So I think we can expect an increase in the level of violence beginning in a few weeks.'

It was now apparent that most of the hardcore al-Qaeda members had departed the battlefield, either in retreat to Pakistan or because they had been successfully targeted by the Coalition Special Forces. However, when Pakistan's army chief, General Ashfaq Kavani, claimed his forces had 'broken the back' of insurgents linked to the Taliban or al-Qaeda, the chairman of the US Joint Chiefs of Staff, Admiral Mike Mullen, was quick to point out that Pakistan's intelligence agency ISI retained ties with the Haqqani network, one of the most active and brutal of the Taliban sects.

In April the Taliban responded with an announcement of its own Operation Badr, a countrywide offensive designed to expand the insurgency in the north. But before the operation gained momentum – if indeed it was anything more than a propaganda exercise – the insurgents suffered the most telling blow of the war. On 2 May, shortly after 0100 hours, a unit of US Special Forces stormed a compound in Abbottabad, about 110 kilometres from the Pakistani capital, Islamabad. The CIA had spent several years tracking al-Qaeda couriers until they were sure they had pinpointed the home of the terrorist mastermind, Osama bin Laden.

Two dozen SEALs from JSOC's Red Squadron flew into Pakistan from a staging base in the city of Jalalabad in eastern Afghanistan in two Black Hawk helicopters modified to fly more quietly and to reduce their radar profile. They were followed part way by two Chinooks carrying 75 additional SEALs as a quick reaction force in case reinforcements were needed.

The flight from Abbottabad took 90 minutes and as they hovered above the target the tail of one helicopter grazed one of the compound's walls. The aircraft rolled on its side but the pilot brought it down in a 'soft' crash landing, which ended with it resting at a 45-degree angle against the wall. The other helicopter landed safely outside the compound and the SEALs scaled the walls then blew the entrances to the house.

As President Obama and his top advisers watched the outside scene from the White House Situation Room, the SEALs advanced through the three floors of the residence, killing three men and a woman before they reached bin Laden's bedroom on the third floor. The al-Qaeda leader peered over the third floor ledge at the Americans charging up the stairs, and retreated into his room. According to the official report, 'As the SEALs approached, bin Laden placed one of his wives between himself and the commandos, pushing her towards them. A SEAL fired several shots at bin Laden's head, and he fell back into his room. Inside the bedroom, bin Laden lay on the floor with a head wound as two of his wives stood over him. One of them, Amal Ahmed Abdul Fatah, screamed at the SEALs in Arabic and motioned as if she were about to charge. One of the SEALs shot her in the leg, then grabbed both women and shoved them aside. A second SEAL entered the room and two SEALs shot bin Laden in the chest. The SEAL team leader radioed, "For God and country, I pass Geronimo, Geronimo E.K.I.A. (enemy killed in action)."' The message went to US Special Operations Commander Admiral McRaven, then directly to President Obama, who said, 'We got him.'

After the raid, US forces took bin Laden's body to Afghanistan for identification, then buried it at sea. Al-Qaeda confirmed the death on 6 May with posts on its favoured websites, vowing to avenge the killing. Other Pakistani militant groups also vowed retaliation, not just against the US, but also Pakistan for not preventing the operation.

Palmer says, 'I was working in the main HQ Ops room when the news broke early in the morning. The Americans were over the moon, and most of the guys who had been there from the beginning felt a sigh of relief – at least I did.

'The next reaction was, "Shit. Now what – who's going to take over as the new Osama bin Laden?" The whole issue was a whirlwind of discussion, but by midday it was over; crack on with business as usual. The Yanks carried on a little for a couple of days; it was, "Yeah, we got him because we knew we could and we knew we would."

'There were many cigars smoked that day!'

The death of bin Laden was also a political milestone. Coalition members had been under increasing pressure to withdraw their forces from an intractable conflict that had no clearly defined exit strategy. Now they were able to set a time line for drawing down their combat troops. By the end of 2014, it was decided that all 150,000 NATO troops would be withdrawn. Australia followed suit, though Prime Minister Julia Gillard pledged that Australian assistance – particularly in military and police training – would continue for a further five years.

'Transition is a gradual process, not an event,' she told the nation in May 2012. '[It is] achieved when the conditions are right on a province-by-province and district-by-district basis.' However, the progress made by the Australian forces in Oruzgan was encouraging and 'Australia's target of completing transition by the end of 2014, and possibly earlier, is on track.'

Australia assumed leadership of Combined Team – Uruzgan (CT-U), including elements from the US, Singapore and the Slovak Republic in late 2012. Its mandate was to secure a smooth transition and to support the Afghan military and civil forces after they assumed responsibility for security in the province. The Australian contingent comprised a headquarters team; a battalion strength 7 RAR Task

Group; a Security Force to provide base security; a provincial reconstruction team for managing development works and a trade training school; an engineering construction unit; a communications team; a number of weapons specialists; and medical personnel at the Tarin Kot hospital.

While the SASR would maintain a watching brief, the regiment would depart Afghanistan with its reputation greatly enhanced. It had suffered four further fatalities since Andy Russell's death in 2002. Many others had been wounded and all carried mental and emotional scars from their time in the front-line. But it had distinguished itself in combat and after Trooper Donaldson's VC in 2008, Corporal Ben Roberts-Smith also received the Victoria Cross for Australia from Governor-General Quentin Bryce at Campbell Barracks on 23 January 2011.

A huge man, 'RS' had been slated for military honours almost from the time he completed selection to the SAS in 2003 as a roommate with Rob Maylor, who would become one of the regiment's top snipers.

On 2 May 2006, Roberts-Smith, now a lance corporal, was a patrol scout and sniper in an observation post near the Chora Pass in Uruzgan when insurgents attempted repeatedly to surround the position. He and another operator left the post to counter the move and in a series of actions he took the initiative to fight off the enemy until air support arrived. He was awarded the Medal for Gallantry.

His VC followed a fierce kill or capture operation in Kandahar Province when, under blistering fire, he exposed his own position to draw attention from his patrol, then stormed the enemy position, killing two machine-gunners. He continued to take the fight to the Taliban forces until they retreated from the battlefield.

The regiment itself was honoured in March 2013 when the Special Operations Command received the first army battle honour since the end of the Vietnam War. It recognised 'outstanding performance' during the Shah Wali Kot Offensive from May to June 2010 by the SAS and 2nd Commando Regiment from the Australian Special Operations Task Group.

The award consolidated public perception of the regiment as the hard cutting edge of Australia's defence force. Since 1984 when he joined the SAS, it had undergone 'monumental' changes, Palmer says. 'We were then living in a world very much in the shadow of Vietnam. And a lot of our methodology was based on the "phantoms of the jungle" era. At that time, to be a successful SAS operative you had to understand the bush; you had to know how to move and live in the field, to understand intimately the natural environment around you, so the emphasis was heavily weighted towards your ability to have refined soldier skills.

'We were still in the old jungle greens. Of course, the SAS had to stand out a little bit, so through our dealings with Americans we were able to purchase the American woodlands pattern camouflage uniform and that was pretty cool. But we only really wore them when we were in the field and around the barracks.

'It was just like the conventional army in a lot of ways and that's fine because this was just on the cusp of the technological explosion – GPS, laser range finders, all these great tools that we have now to assist us. Now, of course, it's a different world. Communications equipment is a major part of that advancement. For many years we were relying on very old technology so we were continuing to fall behind our cohorts globally in the ability to work in operations with them.

'The American Special Forces have been the cutting edge, closely followed by our British friends. The British are very different, though; they have their own style and they're very, very private. That's part of their culture; they've always been that way, as if it's a "need to know" basis. However, when you get into the environment where the top level Special Forces units in the same coalition need to be working on the same plane, it's important to have that link of interoperability or cross-pollination. And there are certain things that you need to share with one another in order to have that, and it's quite difficult with the Brits.

'But what we have set up over the years is exchange programs with people from our equivalent or sister units across the water, and we would obviously learn from what they have available to them from command level back down to tactical level. We've sent officers abroad to interact and learn the way of doing things in a multinational approach.

'We obviously identified the fact that if the SAS was going to be a unit to be reckoned with as a national asset in the future, we had to develop in a way where it was really at the sharp end; and we needed to be able to tap into the resources globally because, as the world became more troubled and there were more hotspots flashing up around the place, there was a higher likelihood that we could be deployed anywhere – not just within our own borders.

'There's been a lot of emphasis on developing skill levels and we had to be self-sufficient enough not to rely on the rest of the Australian army to support us with all the basic stuff that we should need. We had to be able to go to places no matter where they were and have good communications. We needed to have the good weapons systems to be able to not only do the job that we wanted to do but if we had to work with another agency [to be] compatible.'

However, a perennial problem was the regiment's location in Perth and its lack of dedicated aircraft, despite its designation as the Special Air Service Regiment. 'We don't have our own aircraft yet,' Palmer says, 'but they come and pick us up when needed. It's been a point of conjecture for many, many years. Some people say we should move the regiment out of Perth over to where the assets are. The other side say, "Bull – bring the assets to the unit."

'Over the years things have changed, particularly with the big developments in the west, and there's a case for the aircraft to be stationed in Perth and do patrols along the northern coast. Well, Norforce (North-West Mobile Force, an infantry regiment engaged in surveillance and reconnaissance of the remote areas of northern Australia) was born and those units are tasked with all those sorts of things. But we became a far more strategic unit. We developed the counter-terrorist capability, the so-called "black roles".

'In the "black world", that was bubbling on very nicely, we were developing very quickly and trying to be a couple of steps ahead of the bad guys. But the other side of the regiment coin was the conventional SAS "green roles" – the bush, the jungle, boots on the ground, actual eyes on target – all those things that we know as the classical SAS work. So now there was a juggling act within the unit of the Black and Green. We had to come up with a system of how to maintain this capability of counter-terrorism and also maintain our core skills as a unit. And so there was a rotation system.

First of all, there was a trickle system where people in the Sabre squadrons would do the normal, conventional SAS stuff, and then a few at a time would trickle up into the CT environment. People would trickle back from CT to the squadron so there was a constant migration. It worked to a degree, but there was a bit of wastage and the process took a long time.

'So we started looking at the people we recruited. We needed specialists, so perhaps we needed to have university graduates – guys who were intellectually more stable and agile, because things were only going to get more technical as time progresses, even though this really smart stuff is very easy to use. You still need smart people to use it because they understand it and they know how to get the best benefit from it.

'These days, our society as a whole has become better educated; so too are our recruits. Quite a number of diggers in the regiment have got university degrees – some before they come in, some of them after, and they've done postgraduate studies or tertiary studies while still serving in the unit. Language training, higher education is always encouraged. We have a language cell, "Language West", part of the Defence language school at Point Cook, but they have a little detachment in Campbell Barracks that looks after our needs. If we ever need supplementary instructors, they'll come across from Point Cook and help out in the course.

'You want this machine called the SAS to be flexible – to have the capability to be employed anywhere, anytime. To do all these different things which are beyond the scope of any other force or unit you have to put a lot of effort into educating it, developing it, and you have to allow the people themselves to self-improve as well.

'We set up a research and development cell with dedicated people looking at new equipment, new methodologies, new anything that might be an advantage to us. And so, notwithstanding the bureaucratic nightmares that you fight trying to get new equipment through the system, we go through that process to look at new stuff, new ways of doing things, meeting new people, new organisations that might be available to us. You've got to have the drive to push yourself forward. You can't be sitting around because as soon as you stagnate, you fall off, you're out of the race.'

One of the most important aspects is having the capacity to coordinate on the battlefield with Australia's principal ally, the United States. 'We have proven that interoperability with the Americans since we've been involved in Cambodia, Rwanda, Somalia, and more importantly and more recently, Afghanistan,' Palmer says. 'And because we've worked so closely with our Allied friends, we have learned to work with the best technology there is. The leaps that we've taken have been gigantic. We're so far ahead now of where we were 10 years ago. At that time we were a lot further ahead than what the rest of the army was. The gap now has widened. We have been working with the best technology available. That's enabled us to become who we are. The changes have been significant and because of the opportunities that we've been given we've proven ourselves along the way.'

However, while working with the Americans, the ADF and the SAS in particular have followed their own moral values. 'At unit level we're mindful of that moral compass but it's also a job of the politicians to maintain as well because at the end of the day we have to do what we're told. But within that we maintain that moral compass and we understand who we are and what we represent. We can't afford to be embroiled in anything that might dim the reputation or bring us into disrepute. We have our own tradition. The Americans can have theirs.

'We enjoy the Americans because they have all the stuff, but we never compromise who we are.'

25

THE FUTURE

When Clint Palmer left Tarin Kot on 12 July 2011, it was with a sense of satisfaction that he had made an important contribution to the success of the mission. The operations had been completed, albeit with some casualties. The Coalition had made real progress on the battlefield and the al-Qaeda leadership had been decimated. 'We hardly hear of al-Qaeda these days in our operations in Afghanistan,' he says. 'It's all Taliban or insurgents or Pakistanis or a combination of the above.'

But while the Coalition dominated the battlefield, this did not mean the war was won. 'The Taliban now have a political arm that is stepping up and holding negotiations with the government. We all knew this was coming because of the ambivalent way the Americans were doing things.

When they're talking to prominent Afghan leaders it's about needing to negotiate, trying to find peace and political representation. And of course the Taliban leaders are sitting there nodding their heads.

'There was always a political aspect to the Taliban; they're not just a religious sect anymore; this is a full-blown political attack, representing their people as a majority group in Afghanistan. And of course Karzai is changing his tune all the time.'

While he was pleased to have contributed to the fight, there were mixed emotions when he considered his own future. In 2012 he would be 55, and while that had long been the mandatory retiring age for a soldier of his rank, a couple of years previously it had been raised to 60. But there was a catch. 'I could have soldiered on in a full-time capacity for another five years,' he says. 'But I couldn't stay at the regiment because I'd done four years and there were only two positions other than the RSM and I'd had a crack at both of them – two years each. The only way I could stay on was in the big army. But there I'd be competing for an RSM position with guys who were being promoted up; and where was I going to go? I wasn't going to leave Perth because my kids were there.'

He had recognised the problem prior to his deployment to Afghanistan and had discussed it with his CO, Paul Burns. 'I had negotiated an extension,' he says. 'We struck a deal that I would extend by up to two years. But when I was away the COs changed.'

During his brief leave home he had sought an interview with the new man, to confirm the arrangement. He sent emails to the CO's PA about the purpose of the meeting, then arrived as scheduled at the CO's office in Campbell Barracks. 'He welcomed me into his office,' Clint says, 'and then he said, "Now, what was it you wanted to talk to me about?"'

'That was the moment when I knew that this guy wasn't interested at all in me. It was one of those worthless encounters, a complete waste of my time.'

It was a real blow, one that he still has difficulty coming to terms with. 'I felt betrayed absolutely,' he says, 'but such is the beast. There were no grounds for appeal; I had to leave the regiment.' He contacted the section that handles the postings of service personnel. 'I said, "Try to find me a position in WA." Nothing. "Try to find me a position in the Special Operations Command". "Nothing," they said, "you'll have to throw your hat in the ring with all the other WOs in the big army and they'll come up with a job somewhere."' As well as leaving Perth, that would mean he'd be disadvantaged financially. 'So I said, "No, I'm outta here." I took the decision to retire. I transferred from full-time to part-time on 20 February 2012, aged 55 the next day. Midnight on the

20th I got out, so one second later I was 55 and that made me eligible for all my entitlements – pension and payout.'

The suddenness of his departure added to the sense of personal loss. And while there were promises of part-time training work with the regiment, they would soon dry up when Defence cuts in Canberra meant money was tight throughout the ADF. Moreover, he had returned from Afghanistan to a comfortable house provided at subsidised rates by Defence Housing and Callan lived with him while completing his diesel mechanics/heavy machinery apprenticeship. Now, for the first time, he would have to confront Perth's booming real estate market for a home of his own.

Kelsee remained with her mother but visited frequently. He needed to find a place near to his father's old home, but within reasonable distance of his daughter. Callan was planning to take a fly-in, fly-out job with a mining company, and by the time Clint found a suitable location at suburban Quinns Rocks the mining job had come through.

He lived alone.

There was, however, one consolation on the horizon. Since his father's revelation of the family's Aboriginal heritage, Clint had been pursuing the possibility of joining with the clan that gave him such a close and carefree childhood in the bush around Batchelor. He contacted Kathy Deveraux (nee Daiyi), now married to a cattleman far out in the Northern Territory near the Finness River. He researched the Aboriginal

Affairs websites. He learned that despite his own Aboriginal ancestry being based in the Roma district of Queensland, it was acceptable for another clan to include him, provided he met the criteria and they were willing.

He researched his background and plunged into the paperwork. He met the criteria. He sent the results to Kathy, who was his contact point for the other members of the family, particularly her siblings Margy and Richard. In March he wrote that he would be coming to see them in the next few months and suggested she might want to let the others know.

'I'm also keen,' he said, 'to see what the update is on the recognition of Aboriginal heritage which you still have. All the best to the mob and stay in touch.'

The journey back to his stamping grounds was part of the research we undertook for this book. It took us from the Swanbourne headquarters across to Kalgoorlie and then up to Darwin and Batchelor before heading by 4WD through the Litchfield National Park to the big cattle stations now run by Kathy and her close relatives. He and Kathy fished for barramundi in the crocodile-infested Finness River; dingoes crossed our tracks on the way to the two-storey galvanised iron homestead where Kathy's husband Gary told hair-raising (and hilarious) stories of his crocodile hunting days. We stayed with them overnight. 'I feel privileged to have had the exposure to "God's own country" as a boy,' Clint said.

'Is it any wonder that people in the south didn't believe half the stories we used to tell?'

As at the time of writing, Clint believes the situation is still up in the air, with no definite conclusion one way or the other.

Back in Perth, Kelsee came to visit at his Quinns Rock home, where he had begun extensive renovations, including an in-ground swimming pool with a spacious entertaining area. By now he was becoming known in the street and there was a regular inflow of neighbourhood characters.

His father's health was failing, and since his siblings had scattered across the continent he visited daily until it became clear that Terry needed to be moved into permanent care. This meant persuading the old man to make the move, then dealing with the sale of the house and all the bureaucratic arrangements involved in transferring him to the nursing home. Terry lived out his days in a new facility in Huntingdale, sadly passing away on 22 May 2013. He is now laid to rest beside his wife, Isabel.

Over the years in Perth Palmer had established a coterie of good mates, and they met regularly for coffee and occasional camping and fishing trips along the West Australian coastline. And like all his comrades from the regiment, he took a close and continuing interest in the SASR's activities, the course of the war in Afghanistan and the wider war on terror.

He was deeply affected when a good mate, SAS Sergeant Blaine Diddams, was shot dead by a Taliban fighter on 2 July. He had been on a mission to capture or kill a local insurgent leader, 'Najib' Haibat, in the area just north of Tarin Kot. As Sergeant Diddams and his men surrounded the compound, an enemy sniper in a tree fired his rifle and the bullet went through the Australian's shoulder, missing his bullet-proof vest and cutting into his heart. He died instantly. He was 40 years old and the father of two. 'That was really tough,' Palmer says.

The regiment came under unwanted media attention when the Fairfax press reported that a 'secret' SAS squadron had been operating in Africa and had mounted 'dozens of operations in Kenya, Zimbabwe and Nigeria'. According to the report, the regiment's 4 Squadron, 'the existence of which has never been publicly confirmed', had undertaken the missions at the instigation of ASIS, the Australian Secret Intelligence Service.

The government played down the report, but the existence of 4 Squadron, headquartered in Melbourne where ASIS is also located, was an open secret among members of the regiment. I raised the matter in passing with Clint and he refused to comment. Nevertheless, it is clear that it operates in concert with ASIS and its remit covers all potential terrorist threats to Australia. On 19 July, following the press reports, the director-general of ASIS, Nick Warner, broke the public silence of 60 years in an address to the National Press Club in Canberra in which he confirmed the strong relationship that had developed with Australia's Special Forces.

The Bali bombings, he said, together with the 9/11 tragedy had caused ASIS to intensify its focus on 'the very real threat' posed by organisations like al-Qaeda and other extremists. 'As the reach of terrorism has spread, so has ASIS had to expand its collection capability to the Middle East, South Asia and Africa.

'Our work in support of the Australian Defence Force ranges from force protection reporting at the tactical level through to strategic level reporting on the Taliban leadership,' he said. 'ASIS reporting has been instrumental in saving the lives of Australian soldiers and civilians (including kidnap victims), and in enabling operations conducted by Australian Special Forces. The ASIS personnel deployed with the ADF have developed strong bonds, and it's difficult to see a situation in the future where the ADF would deploy without ASIS alongside.' It was as close as the Australian spymaster could come to confirming this developing role of the SAS.

On this larger war on terror, Palmer says, 'Half the battle has been trying to get the support of the public. As far as the majority is concerned there's a conflict going on in Afghanistan. They aren't aware that there's a large force positioned at various bases with their fingers on the pulse, monitoring other hotspots constantly. And they've got 'em sussed. So, why aren't we in Yemen kicking their arse there and really taking it to al-Qaeda, getting them where their roots are and eradicating them? Because if that happened globally, it would be out there; the public would see the Americans all over it. It would be a political issue then – whether the president has the political support to fight more than one war openly.'

In Afghanistan, President Hamid Karzai dances an increasingly complex political minuet as he attempts to assert his independence from the American-led forces in his country, while at the same time ensuring the continued inflow of millions of CIA dollars for his personal use.

In May, 2013 the *New York Times* revealed that the spy agency had been delivering bundles of cash to the presidential palace in Kabul for at least the last decade. CIA sources said the deliveries amounted to millions of dollars, and that no accounting was asked for or received. The revelations caused a storm of criticism in Washington, but Karzai responded that the CIA was 'an easy source of petty cash', and that some of it was used to pay off members of the political elite, a group dominated by warlords.

According to the *New York Times* of 4 May, 'The practice, officials say, effectively undercut a pillar of the American war strategy: the building of a clean and credible Afghan government to wean popular support from the Taliban. Instead, corruption at the highest levels seems to have only worsened. The International Monetary Fund recently warned diplomats in Kabul that the Afghan Government faced a potentially severe budget shortfall, partly because of the increasing theft of customs duties and officially abetted tax evasion. On Saturday, Mr Karzai sought to dampen the furor over the payments, describing them as one facet of the billions of dollars in aid Afghanistan receives each year. "This is nothing unusual," he said.

'He said the cash helped pay rent for various officials, treat wounded members of his presidential guard and even pay for scholarships. Mr Karzai said that when he met with the CIA station chief, "I told him because of all these rumours in the media, please do not cut all this money, because we really need it. It has helped us a lot, it has solved lots of our problems," he added.'

Palmer says, 'The modus operandi of the Taliban has evolved in the last few years; the use of IEDs, suicide bombers and random attacks on public figures is testament to its ability to infiltrate even the highest levels of security within the Afghan Government.

'Afghans live by the family, tribe, clan, creed, and they are reluctant to condemn their own people in the face of the Coalition hierarchy when the elders of the clans or tribes are in the same audience. However, it is plain to see that they do back their own people, even when they know they are Taliban operators, and that they have conducted hostilities against the Coalition. These people will lie through their teeth to save their own skin and to save face with their own people.

'The majority of Afghans don't want Western intervention apart from material things that can make life easier – machinery to plough the fields, medical supplies and communications. Their lifestyle and custom is what makes them Afghans! Corruption is a Western term; to Afghans, it's opportunism – a self-preservation mechanism that helps to keep your enemies at a distance but provide a maximum benefit to you.

'If our power brokers really think or believe that our partnering with these people is the solution, not only are they naive, but totally out of touch with reality. It looks good on the world stage that they and we are taking these very civilised steps to end the conflict in Afghanistan, when in fact it is complicating the scene more than ever.

'The Coalition model for peace may not be the shining light it is promoted to be. Life in Afghanistan will be very dangerous for the small groups of advisers left behind after the main force withdraws. They will be more vulnerable than before. Karzai will either be killed, or he will flee and live in exile.'

It may not be the most charitable or hopeful note on which to end. And it is certainly not the official line of the Australian Government or the SAS Regiment. But it is the sincerely held view of someone who has dealt with the Afghans as both friends and foes, in the front-line of battle and in the daily colloquy of coordination between the Coalition forces and their declared common enemy in the insurgency. It is the unique view of the seasoned soldier whose loyalty is unquestioned and who has never been afraid to deliver his opinions straight from the shoulder.

EPILOGUE

Through all the personal and professional turmoil, Clint Palmer had an abiding dream – to introduce his beloved daughter, Kelsee, to the special excitements and delights of parachuting. When he raised it with her she seemed keen but there always seemed to be some impediment on either side that got in the way. Either he was under the pump at work or she had study or exams that claimed her full attention.

But then, on 19 November 2012, the opportunity literally arose overnight. He called her and, yes, she was up for it. Next day they met at the field. 'Kelsee presents as the strong, silent type,' he says, 'and she maintained that persona right up to when we took off. She pulled the bubblegum out of her mouth and said, "I need to get rid of this". "Too late now," I said, "You'll have to wait till the door opens." The gum went back in the mouth.'

They started the climb to jumping height. Nothing much was said. He'd briefed her thoroughly before they climbed aboard. It was to be a tandem with father and daughter locked together beneath the one parachute. When they reached the optimum altitude and the pilot gave the signal, the door opened and she tossed the bubblegum out as they took up their position.

'She seemed relaxed enough until we rolled out of the aircraft,' he says, 'Then she let out a deafening scream . . . followed by complete silence. When we landed she had a grin like a Cheshire cat and wanted to go straight up and do it all again.' He had arranged for a cameraman to jump with them. 'So she now has the means to relive it,' he says.

'The hug she gave me was all the thanks I needed.'

LIST OF ABBREVIATIONS

ADF	Australian Defence Force
ANA	Afghan National Army
ANP	Afghan National Police
ASC	Australian Services Contingent
ASIS	Australian Secret Intelligence Service
BRA	Bougainville Revolutionary Army
CASO	Complex Adaptive Special Operations
CE	Combat equipment
CPP	Close personal protection
CRA	ConZinc Rio Tinto Australia
CSM	Command Sergeant Major (U.S. Army highest Army enlisted rank)
CT	Counter-terrorism
CUO	Cadet Under Officer

DS	Directing staff
DSO	Distinguished Service Order
DZ	Drop zone
E&E	Escape and Evasion
EKIA	Enemy killed in action
FAM	Fighting aged male
FOB	Forward Operating Base
GHQ	General or Garrison Head Quarters
GPMG	General Purpose Machine Gun
HAPO	High Altitude Parachute Operations
HF	High Frequency
INTERFET	International Force East Timor
ISAF	International Security Assistance Force
ISI	Inter-Services Intelligence (Pakistan)
JDAM	Joint Direct Attack Munition
JSOC	Joint Special Operations Command
JTAC	Joint terminal attack controllers
LRDG	Long Range Desert Group
LRPV	Long Range Patrol Vehicle
LTC	Lieutenant Colonel (US Army)
LZ	Landing Zone
MEAO	Middle Eastern Area of Operations
MFF	Military freefall
MRE	Meals ready to eat
NVG	Night Vision Goggles
OC	Officer Commanding (Squadron/Company Commander)

OCC-P	Office of Centralised Coordination - Provincial
OEF	Operation Enduring Freedom
PMG	Peace monitoring group
RAR	Royal Australian Regiment
RCC	Rescue Coordination Centre
RMC	Royal Military College
RPG	Rocket Propelled Grenade
RSM	Regimental Sergeant Major
SAM	Surface to Air Missile
SAS	Special Air Services
SASR	Special Air Services Regiment
SOLO	Special operations liaison officer
SOTG	Special Operations Task Group
SR	Special Recon
SSM	Squadron Sergeant Major
TACSAT	Tactical Satellite
TAG	Tactical Assault Group
TF	Task Force
TK	Tarin Kot
TMG	Truce Monitoring Group
TNI	Tentara Nasional Indonesia (Indonesian Army)
TOC	Tactical Operations Centre
UNAMET	UN Assistance Mission East Timor
UNTAET	United Nations Transitional Administration in East Timor

NOTES

Chapter One

1 Ian McPhedran, *The Amazing SAS: The Inside Story of Australian Special Forces*, HarperCollins, 2007, p. 147.

Chapter Three

2 Sandra Lee, *18 Hours: The True Story of an SAS War Hero*, HarperCollins, 2006, p. 278.

3 ibid., p. 283.

Chapter Four

4 Gordon Stevens, *The Originals: The Secret History of the Birth of the SAS*, Ebury Press, 2006, pp. 16–20.

5 ibid., p. 63.

6 ibid., p. 76.

7 Fiona McPherson, *Oxford Dictionary of National Biography*, 2004.

8 David Horner, *SAS Phantoms of War: A History of the Australian Special Air Service*, Allen & Unwin, 2002, p. 30.

9 ibid., p. 36.

Chapter Five

10 David Horner, op. cit., p. 130.

Chapter Six

11 David Horner, op. cit., p. 251.
12 ibid., p. 278.
13 ibid., p. 355.
14 ibid., p. 389.

Chapter Seven

15 David Horner, op. cit., p. 393.
16 ibid., p. 437.

Chapter Eleven

17 David Horner, op. cit., p. 460.
18 ibid., p. 461.
19 ibid., p. 462.

Chapter Twelve

20 David Horner, op. cit., pp. 468–9.
21 AM Archive, 24 December, 1999.

Chapter Thirteen

22 Ian McPhedran, op. cit., p 27.
23 ibid., p. 35.
24 Ian McPhedran, op. cit., p. 43.
25 David Horner, op. cit., pp. 491

Chapter Fourteen

26 David Horner, op. cit., p. 509.
27 *Observer*, 2 September 2001.

Chapter Fifteen

28 Ian McPhedran, op. cit., p. 146.

29 ibid., p. 151.

30 ibid., p. 156.

31 Interview with the author, 16 January 2013.

32 *60 Minutes*, 25 April 2004.

33 Sean Naylor, *Not a Good Day to Die: The Untold Story of Operation Anaconda*, Penguin, 2006, p. 22.

Chapter Seventeen

34 Ian McPhedran, op. cit., p. 255.

Chapter Eighteen

35 Rob Maylor and Robert Macklin, *SAS Sniper*, Hachette, 2010, p. 288.

Chapter Nineteen

36 www.dtic.mil/cgi-bin/GetTRDoc?AD=ADA505428.

Chapter Twenty-one

37 Seth G. Jones, *In the Graveyard of Empires: America's War in Afghanistan*, Norton, 2009, p. 328.

38 In November 2012 he resigned as Director of the CIA after revelations of his affair with his biographer.

39 <en.wikipedia.org/wiki> War in Afghanistan#cite note-226.